# Governing Banking's Future

# Innovations in Financial Markets and Institutions

**Editors:**

Robert A. Eisenbeis and Richard W. McEnally
University of North Carolina at Chapel Hill
Chapel Hill, North Carolina, USA

**Other books in the series:**

England, C.; and Huertas, T.:
THE FINANCIAL SERVICES
REVOLUTION

Gup, B.:
BANK MERGERS: CURRENT ISSUES
AND PERSPECTIVES

Kormendi, R., Bernard, V., Pirrong, S., and Snyder, E.:
CRISIS RESOLUTION IN THE THRIFT
INDUSTRY

Hancock, D.:
A THEORY OF PRODUCTION FOR
THE FINANCIAL FIRM

# Governing Banking's Future:

## Markets vs. Regulation

edited by
**Catherine England**

**Kluwer Academic Publishers**
Boston/Dordrecht/London

**Distributors for North America:**
Kluwer Academic Publishers
101 Philip Drive
Assinippi Park
Norwell, Massachusetts 02061 USA


**Distributors for all other countries:**
Kluwer Academic Publishers Group
Distribution Centre
Post Office Box 322
3300 AH Dordrecht, THE NETHERLANDS


**Library of Congress Cataloging-in-Publication Data**
Governing banking's future: markets vs. regulation/edited
  by Catherine England.
        p.      cm.—(Innovations in financial markets and
     institutions)
     ISBN 0-7923-9137-3 (alk. paper).—
     ISBN 0-7923-9160-8 (pbk.)
     1. Banks and banking—United States.   2. Banks and
  banking, International.   3. Banking law—United States.
  I. England, Catherine.   II. Series.
  HG2491.G69   1991
  332.1'0973—dc20                                    90-29325
                                                        CIP

# Contents

I
Overview                                                                                    1

1
Introduction: The Uncertain Future of U.S. Banking                                          3
Catherine England

2
Governing Banking's Future: A View from the Fed                                            11
H. Robert Heller

II
International Coordination of Regulation                                                   19

3
International Regulation: How Much Cooperation Is Needed?                                   21
P. Michael Laub

4
Tension between Competition and Coordination in International Financial                     33
Regulation
Edward J. Kane

Comment on International Coordination of Regulation
Michael C. Keeley                                                                          49

III
Bank Insulation                                                                            57

5
Can Banks Be Insulated from Nonbank Affiliates?                                            59
James L. Pierce

6
Banks Are Not Special: The Federal Safety Net and Banking Powers        79
Walker F. Todd

Comment on Insulating Banks
John H. Kareken                                                         107

Comment on Bank Insulation
Gerald P. O'Driscoll, Jr.                                              111

IV
Payment System Risk                                                     115

7
Daylight Overdrafts: Who Really Bears the Risk?                        117
Robert T. Clair

8
Payment System Risk: A Private-Sector View                             141
Gerard F. Milano

9
The Government's Role in Payment Systems: Lessons from the Canadian     161
Experience
Angela Redish

Comment on Payment System Risk
Mark J. Flannery                                                        181

10
A Proposal to Rely on Market Interest Rates on Intraday Funds to Reduce  189
Payment System Risk
Wayne D. Angell

Index                                                                   197

# Governing Banking's Future

# I OVERVIEW

# 1 INTRODUCTION: THE UNCERTAIN FUTURE OF U.S. BANKING

Catherine England

The U.S. banking industry has seen better days. Questions being asked in mid-1990 about the long-term prospects of U.S. banks are unlike any queries raised since the 1930s. In the spring of 1990, Citicorp, parent company of the nation's largest bank, had its credit rating downgraded by Standard & Poor's and Moody's as a result of concern about real estate losses at Citibank. In fact, no U.S. bank's debt is rated Aaa, and problems with real estate loans, thought at first to be concentrated primarily in New England, now appear to be much more widespread.

The May 21, 1990, issue of *Newsweek* included an article describing the savings-and-loan industry crisis in which the authors ("Bonfire" 1990) warned that "the nation's banks may be next." The article went on to quote several sources who conclude that "the FDIC is effectively broke," a charge Federal Deposit Insurance Corporation officials deny. But on July 16, 1990, a front-page *Washington Post* article (Knight 1990) was head-lined, "FDIC Head Says Fund Is under Stress." No wonder. Though the banking industry averaged only six failures each year between 1945 and

---

The author is director of regulatory studies at the Cato Institute.

3

1979, the average number of annual bank failures jumped to 106 between 1980 and 1989. More than 200 banks failed in both 1988 and 1989, and the costs of resolving those failures led to unprecedented net losses to the FDIC in both years.

At a time when European and Japanese banks are emphasizing expanded international services, U.S. banks are being forced to retrench, to focus on strengthening their capital positions and working out a myriad of domestic loan problems.

There have been numerous attempts to determine the causes of the economic malaise affecting U.S. banks, and there is ample blame to go around. On one point almost everyone agrees: banking law in the United States is out of step with market realities. The regulatory structure erected 50 years ago has been adapted through piecemeal changes wrought by legislated amendments, court interpretations, and regulatory rulings. The result has been described as an "anarchic and disorderly drift" that by its uncertain progress is creating problems for the financial sector and, as a result, for the broader economy as well. There is considerable disagreement, however, on the direction regulatory restructuring should take, especially in the wake of the S&L debacle.

Many observers who blame the S&L crisis on the deregulatory initiatives of 1980 and 1982 argue for stiffer controls over banks and urge caution when others suggest steps that would allow bankers to invest in a broader range of assets or offer an expanded line of financial services.[1] The concerns about losses that may arise if bankers are allowed to enter lines of business in which they are inexperienced are closely linked to questions about the proper extent of the federal safety net—including both federal deposit guarantees and discount window loans from the Federal Reserve System. Whatever one's position on the ultimate desirability of federal deposit insurance, important questions need to be answered before the taxpayers' guarantees are implicitly extended to new industries through bank entry.

Other analysts, including many industry representatives, make the case that risk within the banking industry, and hence risk to the deposit insurance fund, has been significantly increased over the past 15 years precisely because banks are limited in the range of assets they can hold and the types of services they can offer. After all, the roots of the savings-and-loan industry's problems are clearly in regulatory requirements, binding until the early 1980s, that S&Ls fund long-term fixed-rate mortgages with short-term savings deposits. Many bankers argue that they are caught in a similar regulatory bind. As nonbank institutions have created a growing number of securitized debt instruments, those competitors have been able to siphon off the better credit risks—both individuals and businesses—

that had previously formed the banking industry's customer base. Bankers contend that they face significant credit quality problems because regulatory rigidities prevent them from matching nonbanks' financial product innovations. The best customers have been lured away, leaving banks with the customers no one else wants.

Further complicating the debate is a growing awareness of the interdependence of world financial markets. Internationally active banks compete for customers around the world, and a growing number of businessmen no longer limit their searches for new debt or equity capital to their domestic markets. Consequently, major regulatory revisions in one country can have repercussions around the world, and the governments of the industrialized nations have taken several steps to coordinate their regulatory efforts. U.S. bankers note that their competitors in the international arena often have much greater freedom to locate where they choose and to offer a broad array of financial services.

In November 1988 the Cato Institute hosted a conference, "Governing Banking's Future: Markets vs. Regulation," to address issues raised by the changing financial order. The conference was organized in three panels. The first panel discussed the increased interdependence of world financial markets and the resulting pressures for international cooperation among bank regulators. The second panel took up the issue of expanded banking powers by asking whether banks, and hence the federal safety net, can be insulated within broader holding companies. The third panel analyzed risks to the payment system brought about by changes in the financial markets.

Most of the conference papers and comments are contained herein. Given the time that has elapsed since the conference, those papers with analyses or conclusions that have been particularly affected by unfolding events have been updated to reflect relevant new information or conditions.

Federal Reserve Board governor H. Robert Heller opened the proceedings by providing an overview of the growing importance of both international cooperation and questions related to bank insulation. In his article, Heller defends the Federal Reserve's proposed "source-of-strength" policy, through which bank holding companies could be required by the Fed to provide resources to troubled subsidiary banks, and he describes recent efforts to arrive at internationally acceptable capital measures and minimum standards. Heller warns against moves by the Europeans that would tend to insulate their financial markets, and he concludes by calling for changes in U.S. banking laws to provide opportunities for greater geographic and product diversification.

P. Michael Laub and Edward J. Kane specifically address the issues of international regulation. Laub examines three models for international

cooperation—the Basle capital agreement, the financial integration initiatives of the European Community in their march toward 1992, and the
U.S.-Canada free-trade treaty. Though he argues that none of those offers
a perfect model, he identifies the U.S.-Canada agreement as holding the
most promise for productive international cooperation. Laub concludes
that the most viable international agreements will be those that provide
authorities with fundamental controls over the banks operating within their
borders, regardless of where the head office or parent company is located.

Kane's approach to recent international agreements borrows heavily
from cartel theory. He suggests that international efforts at regulatory
cooperation may be attempts by the signatory governments to avoid
competition among their regulatory regimes. Kane warns that, as is the
case with any cartel, such agreements may not be in the best interest of
either covered financial institutions or their customers. On the other hand,
government cartels, like private ones, are subject to erosion over time as
new competitors and potential "banking havens" spring up in countries
that are not party to the agreement and as the signatory nations find they
still compete in terms not explicitly covered by the agreement.

The discussion at the conference then turned to broader asset powers
for banks, focusing specifically on the related question of whether banks
(and hence the deposit insurance fund) can be insulated from potential
losses by affiliated companies. James L. Pierce reviews existing law and
concludes that sufficient protection already exists to allow bank holding
companies to offer a wider range of financial services if bank regulators
have the political will to enforce existing requirements. Though Pierce
suggests that insulation might be strengthened, he also notes that the
ability to insulate banks within holding companies does not necessarily
mean that it is desirable to do so. Pierce describes several drawbacks
to a government-mandated organizational form for financial companies,
including banks, and he emphasizes the important role played by federal
deposit guarantees in increasing the importance of those issues.

Walker F. Todd approaches the issue of insulation by considering the
historic relationship between banks and the federal government. Todd
emphasizes the distinction between a safety net that offers liquidity support
to solvent banks and one that provides capital support to insolvent institutions. He argues that by propping up insolvent institutions (whether banks
or S&Ls) through discount window lending guaranteed by the FDIC, the
federal government has been engaging in socialist credit allocation. Todd
concludes that until we can place effective limits on the growing federal
safety net, it is dangerous to proceed with regulatory restructuring.

The third panel addressed insulation by considering the risks associated with operation of the payment system. Robert T. Clair provides an overview of the U.S. payment system, particularly Fedwire and the Clearing House Interbank Payment System. Clair describes the sources of payment system risk in both systems and then asks who really bears those risks. He concludes that on Fedwire, the risk of substantial losses is ultimately borne by the deposit insurance fund and taxpayers. But, Clair notes, neither taxpayers nor the FDIC has much say about the extent of the risks Fedwire accepts. Clair suggests possible approaches to pricing daylight overdrafts on Fedwire, but he also argues that a phased increase in reserves aimed at allowing the Fed to eventually eliminate daylight overdrafts is worthy of serious consideration.

A private-sector view of U.S. payment systems is offered by Gerard F. Milano of the California Bankers Clearing House Association. Milano also criticizes the close connection between Fedwire's guarantees and the failure resolution practices of the FDIC. Then he asks whether payment system participants really need or require such extensive protection. Milano concludes that much of the payment volume could be eliminated, and the Fed's credit risks substantially reduced, if U.S. banking law allowed nationwide branching and the payment of interest on commercial demand deposits.

Angela Redish describes the Canadian payment system, which is operated by the Canadian Bankers Association rather than by the Bank of Canada. In comparing Canadian and U.S. experience, Redish attempts to discover the theoretical underpinnings of government involvement in the banking system in general and the payment system in particular. Though the differences between the development and operation of Canada's payment system and the U.S. system make it difficult to arrive at any universal truths, Redish does offer a description of a privately operated payment system to contrast with Fedwire.

Federal Reserve Board governor Wayne D. Angell closed the conference. He suggests that the Fed introduce a system for pricing daylight over-drafts as a means of controlling the problem and reimbursing the Fed for some of the credit risk it assumes. Angell's preferred pricing scheme would attempt to encourage an intraday federal funds market by requiring the Fed to charge an above-market rate on overdrafts. He also suggests taking steps to allow Fedwire to operate around the clock. That would provide more timely payment finality for institutions operating in other countries as well as allow less pressing domestic transfers to be conducted in off-peak hours.

The articles in this book offer no clear prescription for revising the U.S. banking laws, but a few important points do emerge. None of the papers is devoted explicitly to federal deposit insurance, but the important role played by the federal safety net is a thread that runs through the entire book. One criticism of international regulatory agreements focuses on their failure to consider the impact of different countries' deposit insurance programs. The debate over the expansion of banks' asset powers basically comes down to the impact of such an expansion on the deposit insurance fund and the impact of banks' deposit insurance on any markets they might enter. Finally, despite the appearance that the Fed bears the risk in allowing daylight overdrafts on Fedwire, the articles herein demonstrate that ultimately it is the federal deposit insurance fund that is at risk. Clearly, any effort at substantive long-term reform must take into account the federal deposit insurance system.

Several authors also note the costs of continuing attempts to segregate the U.S. banking market, both geographically and by product. In continuing such restrictions, the U.S. regulatory regime is increasingly out of step with those of most other countries. Further, limitations on U.S. banks have not only contributed to the risks faced by individual banks, they have also affected the way in which Fedwire has developed and added to the daylight overdrafts generated by its operation.

Finally, it is clear that in the long run the market, increasingly the international market, will drive changes in the U.S. banking system. Technological developments, financial product innovation in both U.S. and foreign markets, and growing competition from financial institutions around the world will ultimately determine the future of U.S. banks. Thus, making changes that will set the U.S. banking industry back on the path to financial stability and avoiding a 1990s banking crisis should be the top policy priorities for the Treasury Department and Congress in the coming year. After all, a healthy, efficient banking sector is a prerequisite for a smoothly functioning, productive economy.

## Note

1. In 1980 the Depository Institutions Deregulation and Monetary Control Act set in motion the elimination of ceilings on deposit interest rates. In addition, explicit deposit guarantees were raised from $40,000 per account to $100,000 per account. Savings and loans, as well as banks, thus became part of a nationwide market in which they bid for insured deposits. In 1982, faced with hundreds of insolvent S&Ls it did not want to close, Congress removed constraints that forced S&Ls to focus primarily on home mortgages. It was hoped that allowing S&Ls to diversify their portfolios would enable them to outgrow existing problems.

## References

"Bonfire of the S&Ls." 1990. *Newsweek*, May 21, pp. 20–25.
Knight, Jerry. 1990. "FDIC Head Says Fund Is under Stress." *Washington Post*, July 16, pp. A1, A5.

# 2 GOVERNING BANKING'S FUTURE: A VIEW FROM THE FED

## H. Robert Heller

No one who studies the history of American banking can fail to be struck by the ever-present tension between market forces and the regulatory presence. In the early years of the Republic, the First and Second Banks of the United States provided an anchor to America's emerging banking system, but many Americans saw those institutions as an anchor that impeded progress, not as one that provided needed stability. Thus, it was no great surprise, when the charter of the Second Bank of the United States expired in 1836, that the nation let the marketplace determine the shape of banking, and a quarter century of free-wheeling banking by state-chartered institutions ensued.

A measure of stability returned when Congress passed the National Banking Act of 1863, although at the time the act was more important as a means of financing the Civil War than as a mechanism for reforming the chaotic banking system. Nevertheless, the legislation established the Office of the Comptroller of the Currency, with the power to charter

At the time of the conference, the author was a member of the Federal Reserve Board of Governors. He is now executive vice president of VISA International.

11

national banks subject to stringent capital requirements, and mandated that circulating bank notes be backed by U.S. government securities.

The Federal Reserve Act of 1913 again provided a central bank for the nation. It also defined the regulatory functions of the Federal Reserve Board. Subsequent legislation further expanded and elaborated the role of the nation's central bank.

## Markets and Regulation

Although I am a supporter of free markets, I am also a central banker. I believe in the constitutional mandate that Congress shall have the power to coin money and regulate the value thereof. Thus, in my view, monetary affairs are the proper realm of government, and the institutions established by Congress to perform financial functions serve a legitimate purpose.

It is also clear, however, that rules and laws should be flexible enough to support the development of markets and not impede their functioning. Flexible rules allow individual financial institutions the leeway they need to adapt to a changing environment so they can meet the financial needs of individuals and corporations.

Rules and regulations also should be equitable to foster fair competition. That qualification applies to domestic as well as foreign institutions that compete in the same marketplace—an important point to which I will return.

The papers in this volume address two important issues: (1) our ability to protect the federal safety net by insulating banks from institutions with which they are affiliated and (2) questions about the international coordination of regulation.

## Insulating Banks

Banks need to be insulated from the economic and financial fortunes of associated activities or affiliated companies because the federal safety net offers special protection for bank depositors. The Federal Reserve's discount window is a ready source of liquidity for banks, and it helps them to avoid being caught short of cash to pay off depositors. Federal deposit insurance offers explicit protection to depositors and is largely responsible for the absence of runs on banks—events that otherwise might not be unheard of in these financially troubled times. In addition to protecting depositors and ultimately taxpayers, legal fire walls between banks and affiliated companies Help to deny those companies access to low-cost funds that might otherwise give them a competitive advantage over companies that are not associated with banks. Insulation is a two-way barrier.

I believe that current laws, especially as embodied in Sections 23A and 23B of the Federal Reserve Act, provide the necessary insulation of banks from their sister companies. But just to be on the safe side, to further protect the banking system and the depositors, the Fed has long adhered to the policy that a holding company should be a source of strength to its subsidiary banks and stand ready to provide additional capital funds in times of financial stress.

### Source-of-Strength Policy

The source-of-strength policy is an important safeguard to the banking system. In its absence, holding companies might well be tempted to ask their banks to remit excessive dividends, charge unwarranted management fees, or engage in other activities that would in effect loot the banks. Especially in times of financial stress, there is no limit to the inventiveness of the human mind when it comes to devising new methods—legal or illegal—of getting money.

Furthermore, if a holding company had the option of cutting loose subsidiary banks that failed to perform up to expectations, true chaos would ensue. Under such circumstances, branch-banking institutions might be tempted to reorganize as bank holding companies with many subsidiaries. Then, as a subsidiary encountered difficulties, it would be allowed to fail, and the Federal Deposit Insurance Corporation would be left to pay off the depositors—while the holding company's shareholders would be left whole. They might even be in a position to walk away with handsome profits from the healthy subsidiaries. Such are the implications of corporate separateness carried to the extreme.

### A Double Umbrella of Protection

I have advocated the double-umbrella concept for bank holding company structure. According to that concept, banks—as well as securities firms, insurance companies, and other financial institutions—could be owned by financial services holding companies. The financial services holding company would have to commit itself to being a source of strength to its bank subsidiary in return for the privilege of owning a bank that has access to the federal safety net and payment system. I would also permit commercial firms to own financial services holding companies, again with the proviso that they serve as a source of strength to the financial services holding companies. Thus, the banking system would have a double umbrella of protection, which could serve to enhance financial stability in periods of economic uncertainty or financial upheaval.

Recently, the Federal Reserve Bank of St. Louis published a study (Gilbert 1988) evaluating the expected effects of a broad range of financial-restructuring proposals on the losses likely to be borne by the FDIC, the rate of return to shareholders as the result of additional diversification, and other factors. According to that evaluation, the double-umbrella concept results in the lowest potential cost to the FDIC and allows shareholders to achieve returns that are only insignificantly lower than the returns that can be obtained under the other alternatives studied.

Let me also mention the Federal Reserve's belief that any operating subsidiaries should be subsidiaries of the holding company, not of the bank itself. There are several reasons for that belief. First, if the subsidiary organization is a subsidiary of the holding company, and not the bank, it is abundantly clear that the federal safety net cannot be used to support the subsidiary if it encounters financial difficulties. Second, in cases in which the parent company might want to come to the assistance of the subsidiary, it would be clear that no funds obtained by the bank at preferential rates could be used to bail out the nonbank subsidiary. That problem would be more likely to arise if the troubled subsidiary were part of a bank with access to funds in federally insured deposits. Third, if a bank subsidiary were to encounter difficulties, those problems would be reflected in the consolidated balance sheet of the bank. Hence, depositors might lose confidence in the bank and fear for the safety of their funds. That dilemma will not arise if the subsidiary is only an affiliate of the bank. Under currently accepted accounting rules, the bank's balance sheet would not reflect the problems of its affiliated institutions.

## International Regulatory Cooperation

Let me now turn to international regulatory issues. Clearly, the ever-increasing integration of financial markets around the world has implications for the coordination of international regulation. In years past there has been relatively little overlap among the various regulatory provinces, but as international banking has expanded and increased in importance, international coordination issues have come to the forefront of the supervisory and regulatory agenda.

I will focus on two issues that have recently received a great deal of attention: the new international risk-based capital requirements and the policy of national treatment versus reciprocity.

### Risk-Based Capital

No discussion of regulatory issues can begin without mention of the new risk-based capital standards developed by the Basle group of bank supervisors and endorsed in July 1988 by the central bank governors of the Group of 10 countries.[1] Although former international supervisory agreements typically relied on reciprocal recognition of national supervisory standards, the Basle group's risk-based capital framework represents the first truly global effort at regulation.

The new framework requires the same definition of capital, the same risk classes, and the same leverage ratio for all internationally active banks. The Basle agreement, as implemented by regulators in the signatory countries, will require banks competing internationally to meet a 4 percent equity standard and an overall 8 percent minimum capital standard by the end of 1992. When considering the capital adequacy of a banking organization, the Federal Reserve Board considers whether the organization meets the new risk-based standard.

### Reciprocity vs. National Treatment

In 1992 the European Community will pass a milestone with the planned full economic and financial integration of the member countries. EC policy toward banks of nonmember countries will be of critical importance to U.S. banks.

There have been recent indications that the European Community may impose a policy of reciprocity on banks of nonmember countries. Specifically, those banks would not be granted the powers available to EC banks unless the same powers were granted to banks of all EC member countries by the foreign banks' home countries. As an extreme example of how that policy might be applied, a U.S. bank could be denied the right to branch throughout the European Community since no banks, domestic or foreign, are allowed to branch throughout the United States. In addition, the securities activities of the U.S. banks in Europe could be restricted because of the restrictions on the securities-underwriting activities of banks in the United States.

Clearly, a policy of reciprocity would be detrimental. Not only would it lessen the ability of U.S. banks to compete in the European market, it could also lead to further protectionist pressures that would be harmful to all. I sincerely hope that the European Community will apply the international standard of national treatment rather than establish a new policy of reciprocity.

## Needed Domestic Reforms

Here in the United States we also need to move rapidly to remove the restrictions that hamper the ability of U.S. banks to compete effectively with foreign financial firms.

For example, greater geographic diversification would enhance the safety of the banking system. That point is forcefully illustrated by the problems encountered by insufficiently diversified banks in the agricultural and energy-producing regions of our country. In sharp contrast, nationwide banking in other countries has increased the safety and soundness of the financial structure through diversification. Although the states have taken the lead in that area, a national policy on interstate banking is clearly needed. The interstate commerce clause, which has brought us prosperity and a competitive marketplace, should be applied to banking as well.

With respect to expanded powers, Congress has unfortunately failed to enact appropriate legislation, and the Federal Reserve Board will therefore be faced with applications from banks requesting new powers within the context of the existing legislation.

## Conclusion

The financial environment we will face in the future is not likely to be much less volatile than that of the past. Further international integration and structural change will occur, and I trust that innovators will be busy. That is the way it should be.

Both regulators and participants in the marketplace should therefore continue to enhance our capacity to cope in a changing environment. The creative forces in the market need to be fostered, and we at the Fed remain dedicated to providing a fair regulatory framework within which the private sector can continue to prosper and flourish.

**Note**

1. The members of the Group of 10 are Great Britain, Canada, Japan, West Germany, France, Italy, Switzerland, Belgium, the Netherlands, and the United States.

**Reference**

Gilbert, R. Alton. 1988. "A Comparison of Proposals to Restructure the U.S. Financial System." Federal Reserve Bank of St. Louis *Review* 70 (July/August): 58–75.

# II INTERNATIONAL COORDINATION OF REGULATION

# 3 INTERNATIONAL REGULATION: HOW MUCH COOPERATION IS NEEDED?

P. Michael Laub

As financial markets have become increasingly international, the question of how competing institutions from different countries should be regulated has been raised repeatedly in many different contexts. I will attempt to address that question by analyzing three recent attempts at coordinating international regulation: (1) the risk-based capital standards developed by the regulators of the major industrial countries, (2) the financial integration initiatives of the European Community, and (3) the financial provisions of the U.S.-Canada free-trade agreement. I will then suggest a framework for cooperation that is, in my opinion, superior to the frameworks used in reaching those agreements.

The framework I would suggest entails three guiding principles: (1) free entry for foreign-owned subsidiaries chartered by the host country, (2) national treatment for all foreign-owned institutions, and (3) national responsibility for all institutions chartered by the host country. That framework will produce a more innovative financial system, more productive interaction among central banks and bank regulators, and safer and more sound banking throughout the world.

---

The author is a private consultant to financial services institutions.

## Purposes of Monetary Policy and Bank Regulation

There probably are as many opinions about the proper purposes of monetary policy and central banks as there are central bankers. However, most observers would agree that, in a general sense, the role of monetary policy is to promote economic stability and that bank regulation is an important tool of that policy. It is widely accepted that in certain unstable situations the failure of an insolvent bank can cause a systemwide panic that leads to the failure of other, solvent banks. Unwarranted systemwide panics can cause great economic disruption by destroying part of the banking system or the money supply. Bank regulation is intended to prevent that from happening.[1]

In a perfect market, with continuously supplied information and perfect liquidity of all assets, a bank could be closed the instant its net worth reached zero. If banks actually were closed when their net worth reached zero, there would be no need for capital requirements or insurance fund reserves, and depositors would, in effect, have 100 percent insurance. Capital requirements, insurance fund reserves, and many other forms of bank regulation exist because of the impossibility of continuously by and perfectly monitoring net worth, the lack of perfect liquidity of assets, and incomplete knowledge about the true long-run equilibrium values of assets, particularly in a problem-bank situation.

In countries with credible deposit insurance systems, systemwide panics should not develop among insured depositors. In spite of the impossibility of obtaining absolutely complete information, it is possible to imagine depositors having enough information to adequately monitor banks and accurately assess the value of depository assets. If such is the case, and if the banking system is sound, a systemwide panic should not develop under any circumstances. If a systemwide panic does develop, the central bank can provide liquidity to private banks so that an orderly determination of asset values can be made and a "fire sale" of bank assets, which could drive down market values systemwide, can be avoided. Ultimately, only central banks, not deposit insurance funds, can provide such liquidity. That is so because central banks are the only institutions that can create their own reserves.

## Problems Caused by the Evolution of the Financial Services Industry

The financial services industry is undergoing revolutionary changes. Securities are traded worldwide 24 hours a day, mutual funds are investing in stock and bond markets thoughout the world, credit cards are accepted everywhere, and domestic corporations and governments are issuing securities in foreign markets. The most important cause of those changes is the decline in the cost of accessing and using information, a particularly important development for the information-dependent financial services industry.

Economic changes are also forcing a restructuring of the financial services industry. Internationalization of markets for both real and financial goods and services is the most fundamental of those changes; the volatility of equity prices, interest rates, and commodity prices is also increasing risk as markets transcend national boundaries. Greater wealth and personal income in many countries have accentuated the economic changes that, combined with the technological changes mentioned above, have been the driving forces behind internationalization.

Finally, demographic changes have been an important stimulus for innovations in the financial services industry. Many countries have been experiencing an increase in the proportion of their populations in older age groups. Those people have special financial needs, including greater retirement savings and means of paying for increased medical care. In developing countries, higher literacy rates, as well as the increasing financial sophistication of the more educated segments of society, have increased the demand for financial services. In addition to those demographic changes, the people in most countries have increasingly come to understand the internationalization of markets and recognize its advantages—more competitive prices, a broader range of higher quality products, and a general increase in standards of living as the result of specialization and trade.

Those trends have led regulators everywhere to recognize that isolated national markets, particularly in financial services, are a thing of the past. The argument heard with increasing frequency is that regulatory functions can only be performed well if all regulatory systems are made uniform, or at least "harmonized." Regulators in countries that have different institutional histories and structures are facing consumers and businesses who are dissatisfied with traditional regulatory boundaries. Domestic constituents are demanding more sophisticated products and services from their financial institutions and are willing to buy them from anyone who will provide quality service at a reasonable price. "Harmonization" is difficult to define and achieve, but the market will not wait.

The following analysis indicates that, so far, attempts at international cooperation leave much to be desired. The alternative framework that I will suggest offers more flexibility and responsiveness to changes in market conditions yet allows national regulators to follow the traditions and rules that work best in their own local markets.


## Recent Attempts at International Cooperation

### Risk-Based Capital Standards

The formulation of risk-based capital standards began with discussions between representatives of the Bank of England and the Board of Governors of the Federal Reserve System, who were concerned about the internationalization of capital markets and the increase in off-balance-sheet activities. The discussions were also prompted by British and American bankers who were anxious about what they perceived as unfairly low capital standards applied to Japanese banks. After a critical level of agreement had been reached, the 10 major industrial countries—the United States, Great Britain, Canada, Japan, West Germany, France, Italy, Sweden, Belgium, and the Netherlands—began cooperatively to develop common capital standards for internationally active banking institutions. Clearly, concern about the competitive success of Japanese banks was a motivating factor in the participation of many of those countries.

The cooperative effort began at the staff level. Once the necessary compromises and accommodations had been achieved at that level, presentations were made to the domestic regulators or legislative bodies, or both, of the participating countries. Input was gathered from the various national constituent groups, and after further arduous negotiations and compromises additional changes were made. In the presentations to regulators and legislators, heavy emphasis was placed on the idea that, because of the arduous negotiations that had produced them, the proposals should be accepted or rejected as a package. In fact, the drafters of the proposals explicitly agreed that national regulators could only make the standards more stringent; they could not liberalize them.

A two-tiered capital system was adopted by the drafters of the risk-based capital standards. Equity capital and disclosed reserves are the main elements of the first tier; the second tier consists primarily of other forms of reserves, hybrid debt-equity instruments, and subordinated debt. Tier-one capital elements must account for at least half of a bank's total capital, and subordinated debt may amount to no more than 50 percent of tier-one capital. A risk-weighting system was adopted to define adequate capital. Under that system various asset categories are given risk weightings of

0, 20, 50, and 100 percent. Mortgages are weighted at 50 percent, but all other strictly private claims and instruments held by banks (i.e., instruments that have no government guarantees attached to them) are weighted at 100 percent. Thus, there is virtually no attempt to distinguish among the risks associated with different types of private-sector claims.

There are several problems with that approach to international cooperation. The first is the difficulty of attaining international uniformity. The differences among the regulatory systems of the major industrial countries are significant. In some countries the relations between banks and their regulators are distant and formal. In others they are informal and cozy. Some countries use specific laws and regulations to influence bankers' behavior. Others use personal contact and moral suasion to a much greater extent. Such differences often arise from deeply embedded cultural differences, and it is not clear that there is much to be gained by attempting to force all banks into a common mold. We can expect cultural differences to influence the implementation of internationally agreed-upon standards and make their absolutely uniform enforcement unlikely. An even more fundamental problem has to do with the extent of the safety net provided by the various central banks to protect domestic activities and institutions. Although safety nets protect different things in different countries, no country is willing to explicitly delineate the limits of its safety net. Cooperation on capital standards but not safety nets, especially their use to protect banks' international operations, will lead to muddled market perceptions.

A third major problem is that judgments about proper or acceptable risks will inevitably became politicized. Conflicts will occur when risky activities are deemed socially desirable. Two examples that have caused problems for the U.S. regulatory system are Third World lending and housing. In the early 1980s banks realized that loans to Third World countries were becoming more risky. Bank regulators, of course, also knew that those loans represented increasing risk. The chairman of the Federal Reserve Board nevertheless continued to encourage more Third World lending. A similar situation arose in real estate lending in the early 1970s. Real estate investment trusts were hailed by regulators as a new vehicle banking companies could use to support politically desirable forms of lending. When the new vehicle got into trouble, regulators did an about face. The potential for that type of regulatory arbitrariness is greatly expanded under a system of risk-based capital.

Furthermore, because its standards are focused on the risks of particular activities or investments, the risk-based system ignores many of the most important tools of risk management—diversification, use of futures contracts as hedging devices, interest rate swaps, and other derivative instruments. The standards also fail to take into account other methods of controlling risk, such as the use of corporate separateness to isolate risky activities in subsidiaries and the imposition of market risk on uninsured depositors and creditors, which leads to direct market discipline of financial institutions.

If a system of risk-based capital is to make banks pay an implicit price for taking more risk, the number and types of risk categories and the way in which overall risk is measured must be refined. Such refinement will inevitably cause more controversy and lead to greater political pressures on the regulators to protect and promote certain favored types of lending. There is an inherent conflict whenever political agents attempt to define and set a price on risk. Why should regulators be presumed to be better than the market at judging proper risks? It is more probably the case that politically influenced judgments made by government regulators about the proper risk weights for different asset categories will not take into account marketplace needs or realities.

The domestic and international integration of the financial services industry means that risk-based capital standards will have important effects on nonbanking financial industries. The agreed-to standards entail higher overall capital requirements for banks as well as risk weightings of bank assets. Those higher capital ratios will tend to force financial activities outside banking institutions, thus promoting the nonbank portions of financial industries worldwide. If corporate separateness is accepted and capital requirements are placed only on the bank portions of holding companies, banking companies may continue to fare relatively well. However, if capital requirements are placed on entire bank holding companies, or if nonbank financial activities are conducted inside banks, as they are in West Germany, the greater capital requirements will put banking institutions at a disadvantage relative to less regulated competitors. Each country will weigh the importance of those effects differently. That is as it should be. Hence, it is argued below that a better approach to cooperation would be to agree on freedom of entry and national responsibility for the activities that are allowed in each country.

## Financial Integration of the European Community

As part of its efforts to achieve full economic integration by 1992, the European Community has announced a tentative plan for integrating its financial institutions. The key provision is a single banking license that will permit a bank from one country to open branches in any other EC member country and still be governed by the regulations of its home country. Common rules on capital adequacy for banks will extend to all EC members. Controls on short-term capital flows will be abolished. Residents of any member country will be able to open bank accounts in any other EC country. Barriers to cross-border marketing of financial services will be lifted, and an attempt will be made to devise a single payment system. Banking firms from outside the European Community will be subject to a policy of reciprocity. That is, a bank chartered outside the European Community will not be allowed to enter a member country unless the bank's home country grants EC banks entering its markets the same privileges they enjoy in their home markets.

There are several problems with the European approach. Essentially, the EC countries are saying that they are unable to determine a common basis on which banks of member countries should be allowed to compete. Because of the strong desire for integration, the European Community has adopted an approach that will allow every bank to compete in all markets and let each individual country decide whether the results indicate that it should change its regulatory system.

As long as there is general stability in the banking system, banking organizations that operate under the least burdensome domestic regulatory systems will grow fastest. The fastest growing banks will probably be the universal banks of countries such as West Germany. Regulators in other countries will come under intense pressure to refashion their regulatory systems along the lines of the universal banking system. Regulators who lack experience with that system will inevitably make mistakes. Because of the single banking license, banks that branch throughout Europe will be regulated by their home countries and the results of those mistakes will not be confined to a single country. They will spread to all countries where a troubled bank does business, and governments of the "infected" countries will have very little recourse.[2] If failures do occur, depositors will be required to spend more time and resources evaluating the effectiveness of a multitude of regulatory systems. Such problems could disillusion and confuse some depositors.

Perhaps the worst part of the proposal for European integration is the requirement that reciprocity be applied to banks domiciled outside the European Community. Reciprocity is an attempt to force European regulatory systems on foreign countries. Countries that are not EC members will either conform to the European system as it emerges, or their banks will be forced to withdraw. The United States and Japan clearly are the major targets of that provision. If enforced as currently proposed, the provision would also encourage European banks to look inward and could result in balkanization of the international financial system.

## The U.S.-Canada Free-Trade Agreement

The recently negotiated free-trade agreement between the United States and Canada (signed into law by President Reagan on September 28, 1988) also covers financial institutions and cross-border investments, but the provisions of that agreement point in a more productive direction than do those of the other two attempts at international cooperation. The United States has agreed that all domestic and Canadian-chartered banks in the United States will be permitted to underwrite and deal in securities backed by Canada or its political subdivisions. The United States also has agreed that it will not invoke any federal law to diminish the ability of Canadian banks to operate in more than one state. Any liberalization of Glass-Steagall restrictions applied to U.S. banks will automatically apply to Canadian banks operating in the United States as well.

Canada has agreed that U.S. firms and investors will be exempt from restrictions on foreign ownership of Canadian financial institutions. U.S.-controlled Canadian bank subsidiaries will be exempt from size limits imposed on other foreign bank subsidiaries. Subject to prudential supervision, U.S.-controlled bank subsidiaries will be able to transfer loans to their parents. The Canadian government has also agreed that it will not use its power to control entry in a manner that is inconsistent with the provisions of the treaty.

The treaty also contains several provisions related to investment powers that should enhance the health of the financial services industries in both countries. Each country is committed to providing investors of the other "treatment no less favorable than that accorded in like circumstances to its [domestic] investors." Enumerated performance requirements as a condition for investment in either country's territory are prohibited. Property may not be expropriated without due process. Finally, restrictions on the transfer of earnings, except for purposes of complying with bankruptcy, tax, and securities laws, are prohibited.

The importance of the agreement between the United States and Canada lies less in its specific provisions than in the positive direction it establishes. Unlike the other two attempts at international cooperation, it is not designed to achieve uniformity of regulation. Instead, it seeks to secure freedom of entry while preserving the regulatory prerogatives of the host country.

## Summary

Risk-based capital standards presume a need for common capital standards across countries. The details of forging an agreement were left to the staffs of the primary bank regulators in each country, and compromises were inevitable. Although domestic constituencies' reactions to the proposals were invited, the arduous negotiations that led to the proposals generated intense pressure on the principals not to make changes.

The European Community's approach to financial integration seems to be driven by a political desire to achieve an integrated market within Europe, despite significant institutional differences among countries. Underlying that desire is a belief that the market pressures that result from different regulatory systems operating in the same market will produce the right answer.

The financial provisions of the U.S.-Canada free-trade agreement take a direction that, in my judgment, is more productive. The provisions are more limited in scope than are those of the European initiative. National treatment and national sovereignty are preserved. However, the delicate issue of national responsibility for failing institutions, and its relationship to monetary policies, is not addressed.

## A Better Alternative

A productive basis for international regulation can be formulated around three principles:

1.  free entry for foreign-owned subsidiaries chartered under the laws of the host country;
2.  national treatment for those subsidiaries; and
3.  national responsibility for (a) monetary policy, (b) prevention of unwarranted financial panics in domestically chartered institutions, whether foreign or domestically owned, and (c) supervision of all domestically chartered institutions, regardless of ownership.

Such a system would preserve national sovereignty yet prevent discrimination against foreign institutions. Logically, it would mean an end to branch systems supervised by foreign examiners. It would also mean that regulators would be required to accept the principle of corporate separateness as a regulatory tool.[3]

The system I propose would not end the differences in regulation and allowable activities that exist among different countries. It would only rationalize them. To the extent that one country's system created a more favorable regulatory climate, financial activity would tend to take place in that country, unless disruptions and panics demonstrated that what appeared to be a favorable climate was, in fact, unfavorable. Under such a system, it would be more difficult for disruptions and panics to spread across national borders, but countries would still have the opportunity to learn from each other's accomplishments and mistakes.[4]

## Conclusion

At first glance, international cooperation in the regulation of financial institutions seems to be desirable. Closer scrutiny reveals, however, that some types of cooperation can force counterproductive regulatory change. Some of the current attempts at international cooperation are leading in that direction, and they could cause trouble for domestic regulators in the years ahead. Most of the differences in the regulatory systems of different countries arose for reasons that undoubtedly seemed sound at the time. The internationalization of financial markets probably has not changed all those reasons. Hence, attempts at cooperation that seek to impose a uniform regulatory system on all countries will inevitably lead to conflict. The alternative framework presented here will preserve maximum flexibility for individual regulators while allowing internationalization to continue in a fair and prudent manner. It is a better way to proceed.

## Notes

1. Of course people have at various times suggested other reasons for bank regulation. Some of those include consumer protection, preventing undue concentration of power, and protecting the integrity of the payment system. With regard to the first two reasons, bank customers would seem to need no more protection than that offered under the general consumer protection and antitrust laws. Payment system problems were a cause of major systemwide panics before World War II. Since then they have not been the cause of such panics, although many observers have suggested that they could be. If the third reason is still valid, it should be recognized that the underlying rationale is still the prevention of unwarranted systemwide panics.

2. The logical equivalent of that situation in the United States would occur if state-chartered depository institutions that were not subsidiaries of holding companies had the power to branch anywhere in the country and only the states in which they were chartered retained regulatory authority over them. Thus, for example, if California thrifts were given very liberal investment powers, as they recently were, and those powers caused the depository

institutions that exercised them to become insolvent, as some have charged is the case, the institutions could still branch anywhere in the United States and other states would have no recourse.

3. The principle of corporate separateness means that if two or more corporations are affiliated and one of them encounters difficulties, there is no legal obligation on the part of the others to come to the rescue. Regulators who use separateness as a tool to promote stability will not allow one bank to come to the aid of a second bank or a nonbank affiliate within the same holding company if such assistance would endanger the first, presumably healthy, bank. Using separateness effectively is not overly burdensome or complex. The most important requirement is that regulators believe in separateness and stand willing to enforce it. If they do not believe in its efficacy, or require overly restrictive fire walls because of their lack of confidence in separateness, the system will not work. See Samuel Chase & Company (1983) and Chase, Laub & Company (1987).

4. In a broad sense, the benefits of the proposal are not unlike those that have accrued to the United States from its dual banking system. See Chase, Laub & Company (1988).

## References

Chase, Laub & Company. 1987. "Insulating Banks from Risks Run by Nonbank Affiliates." Paper prepared for the American Bankers Association, Washington, D.C., October.

Chase, Laub & Company. 1988. "Benefits of the Dual Banking System." Paper prepared for the American Bankers Association, Washington, D.C.

Samuel Chase & Company. 1983. "Corporate Separateness as a Tool of Bank Regulation." Paper prepared for the American Bankers Association, Washington, D.C.

# 4 TENSION BETWEEN COMPETITION AND COORDINATION IN INTERNATIONAL FINANCIAL REGULATION

### Edward J. Kane

Popular discussions of financial regulation naively ascribe to financial regulators remarkable powers and heroically idealistic goals. If such powers and goals are indeed real, it is hard to understand why regulation so regularly goes awry. If superpowered public servants seek only to promote the common good and are able to perceive that good in a miraculously clearsighted fashion, how can they fail?

In contrast, microeconomic critiques of financial services regulation assume that regulators have inadequate tools and feet of clay. Microeconomists see regulators as self-interested individuals laboring in an uncertain and conflictive environment that imposes many important restraints on what any particular regulatory enterprise can even hope to accomplish. Hidden agendas and slips between regulatory intentions and achievements are the norm. Regulatory performance is routinely compromised by avoidance behavior of regulatees and by conflicts in regulatory objectives.

---

The author is Everett D. Reese Professor of Banking and Monetary Economics at Ohio State University.

Microeconomic analysis of financial regulation has two key elements. First, managers of individual regulatory entities seek to maximize something broadly equivalent to the value of their enterprises, subject to technological, market, and statutory restraints and principal-agent difficulties. Second, individual regulatory enterprises are in competition with each other for whatever it is they maximize (Scott 1977). A regulatory agency's objectives may entail tradeoffs among the quality of its performance; its managers' narrow career interests; and its jurisdiction, its budget, or some form of what we may call its net "tribute."

The microeconomic view implies that the interests of regulators and their regulatory clientele are to some extent intertwined (Stigler 1971). It also implies that the producers of financial regulatory services constitute an industry, the members of which establish an equilibrium market structure (Kane 1988). Members include private self-regulatory associations and state, federal, foreign, and international bureaus. We may envision those entities as continually considering adjustments in the services and regulatory burdens they offer, in hopes of winning regulatory business away from each other. We may also envision their managers as occasionally getting together in smoke-filled rooms to investigate possibilities for negotiating various kinds of cartels.

Consumers, who instinctively fear private cartels and support laws to control them, naively view with approval intra- and intergovernmental efforts to monopolize regulatory markets. Such efforts, which are marketed to the public as "harmonization," "cooperation," and bureaucratic "steamlining," are not subject to ordinary antitrust restrictions.

Pursuing the microeconomic view of regulation, this paper emphasizes that regulatory cooperation is fundamentally cartellike behavior. A private cartel constrains member firms to behave in ways that broadly maximize the joint profits earned by its membership. Similarly, a regulatory cartel constrains regulators in different jurisdictions to maximize some joint objective function. However, differences in the effective regulatory incentives of member agencies make the cartel's objective function difficult to summarize.

Any cartel can foster socially harmful distortions, and its stability can eventually be undermined by the competitive pressure it seeks to curb. During the life of a cartel agreement, competitive pressure tends to cause competitors to do business with outside suppliers and engage in activities that the cartel agreement fails to cover adequately.

To clarify the cartel analogy, I examine two developing and widely celebrated international regulatory accords: (1) the risk-based capital agreement and (2) the European countries' drive to unify their financial services markets. The analysis seeks to show that, whatever their benefits, those still-evolving agreements can have undesirable short- and long-run effects. They can conceal or foster serious weaknesses in individual countries' regulatory tactics and strategies in the short run (such as deposit insurance subsidies to risk taking) and can intensify international regulatory competition in the long run. The bottom line is that consumers should be every bit as wary of governmental cartels as they are of private ones. That is true even though, in the long run, the equilibrium character of international regulation depends far less on the vagaries of intercountry regulatory agreements than on the pressure generated by market forces that inevitably act to penalize inefficient uses of resources.

## Competition among Financial Regulatory Systems

In the financial services market, the perceived quality of a firm's products depends on customers' opinions of their convenience and the degree of confidence customers have in them.[1] Confidence and convenience are relative concepts that are based on explicit comparisons of alternative suppliers and the smoothing of connections forged in repeated chains of transactions. They are dependent on the way a firm fits into an efficient and reliable system of trading and transactions. Connections with a system and credible comparisons of firm quality can be produced more efficiently (i.e., at lower cost) with the help of a reputable outside party than they can on a stand-alone basis.

For this reason economic efficiency requires that financial services be produced jointly with external regulatory services. Financial regulatory services consist of private or governmental efforts to monitor, discipline, or coordinate the behavior of individual financial services firms to achieve economic efficiency and other societal goals. In competing with private regulators, governmental entities benefit from the "capital" of the state's reputation. That capital adds weight both to such an entity's specific financial resources and to the explanatory claims its managers make.

To portray financial regulation as a market-driven process, it is necessary to draw a correspondence between the concepts featured in theories of market behavior and various kind of regulatory activity. Although the jurisdictions of a country's financial regulators typically overlap to some extent, one can usually identify a dominant regulatory firm. In many countries the dominant firm is the central bank. The central bank's ability to enter any regulatory submarket in emergencies and to evoke top-level government support for its actions often permits it to impose a degree of cartellike discipline on other members of its country's domestic financial regulatory industry. However, like dominant firms in any domestic market, a country's dominant financial regulator must worry about foreign competition (Giddy 1984).

Changes in regulatory market structure typically originate in regulatee arbitrage of regulatory differences or in supply-side innovations in pricing, production, financing, and marketing by foreign regulators or nondominant domestic suppliers of regulatory services. Innovations in pricing change the pattern of the implicit or explicit charges or subsidies that a given regulator establishes for its clients. Examples include changes in reserve requirements and the Federal Reserve's decision in 1980 to maintain promotional below-cost fees for its electronic clearing and settlement services. Innovations in production can change both the quality of the services a regulator produces and the explicit and implicit costs of producing those services. The Federal Reserve's repeated modernization of its clearing and settlement system is an example of innovation in production. Innovations in financing reduce at least the explicit costs of financing an agency's unfunded expenditures. Such innovations can best be exemplified by the economically insolvent Federal Saving and Loan Insurance Corporation's (FSLIC's) creative use of a financing subsidiary and contingent debt to keep itself liquid. Innovations in marketing are intended to change public perceptions of the need for regulation and of the effectiveness of rival suppliers. The most notable marketing efforts of the last few years have been those of securities and futures regulators to blame defects in each other's systems for the stock market crash of October 19, 1987.

In analyzing regulatory innovations, it is helpful to conceive of individual regulatory entities as multiproduct firms and to employ the "imperfectly contestable markets" paradigm of Baumol, Panzar, and Willig (1986). A market may be defined as a body of persons who engage in extensive and at least partly voluntary transactions that involve a specific good or service. Baumol et al. define an individual market as "perfectly contestable" when the costs of entering or exiting that market are zero. In a perfectly contestable market, the threat of hit-and-run entry by potential competitors from outside can be counted on to hold the profit margin sought by incumbent firms to competitive levels, regardless of the number of incumbent competitors or of how great the share of industry output produced by the few largest competitors happens to be.

Markets for regulatory services are demonstrably *not* perfectly contestable. There are significant exit costs. Because of their ability to conceal implicit losses, government regulators can zealously resist exit, no matter how economically unprofitable their operations may become. Regulatees that try to switch to a new supplier of regulatory services often incur substantial transition or switching costs. Current efforts to prevent well-capitalized thrifts from leaving the insolvent Federal Savings and Loan Insurance Corporation and its successor insurance fund exemplify how explicit exit fees, administrative delays, and outright prohibitions can be used as policy instruments for preserving the market share of an inefficient regulator.

The market structure for financial regulatory services is characterized by dominant firms, influenced by market power conferred temporarily on elected politicians, and distorted by various subsidies the politicians deliberately or inadvertently give to firms that sign up for specific types of regulation.

For many years federal bank regulators in the United States sought to build walls between different types of financial services firms (such as banks, securities firms, and insurance companies) and between the geographic markets served by deposit institutions. During the last 25 years those walls have been undermined by technological change and by competition from foreign and state regulators. Erosion has also occurred in the barriers to entering related financial services fields and in the distance-related costs of running complex interregional businesses. Those declines have made it increasingly less costly for financial firms to penetrate U.S. and foreign regulators' administrative fences by cleverly adapting their institutional structures to squeeze through loopholes in the system of prohibited activities.

The recent global acceleration of financial and regulatory change reflects the response of regulatees and regulators to exogenous and endogenous decreases in the costs of entry into and exit from various financial product markets. The microeconomic view is that product line and geographic market expansion by suppliers of financial regulatory services follow and support rivalry between client financial services firms within and across countries, regions, and various kinds of administrative boundaries. Supplementing strictly bureaucratic theories of regulatory behavior (e.g., Niskanen 1971), my conception is based on the premise that regulators attempt, subject to bureaucratic, market, and technological constraints, to extend or to defend their share of the market for regulatory services in the face of exogenous and endogenous disturbances in the economy.

From the point of view of a regulatee, revenue losses imposed by a given regulator's explicit charges and various operational constraints reduce the net value of the regulatory services received. I define the difference between the costs and benefits that a given regulator imposes and confers on an individual regulatee as that regulatee's "net regulatory burden."

Because that met burden is the counterpart of the regulator's price for its regulatory services, in a competitive market for regulatory services it would be subject to the law of one price. Around the world today, capital regulation, geographic restraints, and restrictions on activities are the cutting edge of regulatory burdens and of the equalizing effect of regulatory competition.

## The Group of 10's Risk-Based Capital Agreement

Central bankers in industrial countries have complained long and loudly about differences in the capital adequacy standards enforced by different nations. They see differences in the burden of capital requirements as an important source of competitive inequality for multinational banks.

Using the Bank of International Settlements in Basle as a forum, representatives from the central banks of the Group of 10 (G-10)[2] agreed in December 1987 as a matter of principle to adopt

1. *a common definition of banks' eligible capital*, that is, a shared framework for measuring an individual bank's capital resources, and
2. *a common minimum standard for capital adequacy*, that is, a minimally acceptable ratio of eligible capital to the aggregate risk exposure that is inherent in an individual bank's business.

To ease the transition to the new definition and adequacy standard, the agreement allows individual countries five years for adjustment. During the transitional period, and to some degree even thereafter, countries may retain some features of their traditional regulatory standards and measurements.

### Procedures for Calculating Capital Adequacy

The Basle accord answers three questions: (1) What are the relevant risks a bank faces? (2) What elements of a bank's capitalization should authorities account as a buffer against those risks? (3) What balance should a bank be made to strike between its risk exposure and its regulatory capital?

The answers provided by the G-10 framework are based on a five-part categorization of risks and the book values of common equity, capital reserves, and specific categories of nondeposit debt. It is convenient to begin with the definition of eligible capital. Capital is divided into two tiers.

"Core capital" is the book value of the sum of common equity and reserves accumulated from retained earnings. "Supplementary capital" has five components:

1. so-called hidden reserves, which constitute formally undeclared earnings that the regulatory framework of a given country accounts as capital;
2. revaluation reserves, which specifically include unrealized gains on a bank's investments in corporate equities (such reserves are particularly important to Japanese banks);
3. general provisions and general loan loss reserves, which are defined as loss reserves not ascribed to particular assets and not considered as earmarked reductions in the value of particular assets (such reserves are important to U.S. banks);
4. hybrid debt-capital instruments, which constitute an open-ended category for contracts in which the debtholder must support losses without being able to trigger liquidation (e.g., long-term preferred stock, perpetuities, and mandatory convertible debt); and
5. subordinated term debt, which is separated from the previous category by its capacity to absorb losses only in the event of liquidation.

The components of supplementary capital are then tempered by miscellaneous deductions for goodwill and investments in unconsolidated financial subsidiaries. Additional deductions are authorized for countries that wish to impose them.

The minimum capital standard is based on a five-part weighting system for assessing a bank's risk exposure. Authorized weights are limited to 0, 20, 50, and 100 percent and apply to broad categories of assets and off-balance-sheet positions. In effect, a bank's relevant risk exposure is measured as a weighted aggregate of the value of various parts of its business. The agreement declares that the ratio of eligible capital to exposure must meet a target of 8 percent. Core capital must represent at least half of that amount, or a minimum of 4 percent of a bank's capital. Various limits are also placed on individual components of supplementary capital.

## Loopholes in the G-10 Framework That Conceal and Support Harmful Distortions

Pearce (1986, p. 57) defines a cartel as "a formal agreement between firms in an oligopolistic market to cooperate with respect to agreed procedures on such variables as price and output." He emphasizes that sanctions and side payments must generally exist to induce cartel members to adhere to those procedures. Economists have always been interested in underscoring the welfare losses caused by cartels and in identifying conditions that are apt, in time, to weaken or disrupt such agreements.

The biggest loophole in the G-10 regulatory framework is its application to "banks" rather than to generic "financial services firms." That loophole leaves room for lobbyists in the United States to influence decisions about what is and what is not a bank and whether and how to consolidate subsidiary and affiliated firms. Those decisions may result in an unintended redistribution of regulatory burdens. The second-biggest loophole is the focus on the book value of a bank's eligible capital rather than on the market value of equity funds contributed explicitly or implicitly by stockholders and debtholders. To the extent that accounting gimmicks permit a bank to raise the book value of its capital position above the market value of that position, the firm's regulatory burden can be effectively ameliorated.

Additional weaknesses lie in using arbitrary rather than market-based measures of a bank's assets and off-balance-sheet risks, subjecting the introduction of new categories of risk to bureaucratic and negotiatory lags, papering over tough issues by granting individual countries a series of options that allow them to deviate from the common standard, and neglecting individual firms' continuing options to relocate or restructure their businesses in ways that exploit residual differences among the signatories or larger differences between the G-10 countries and other regulatory venues.

Industry opposition to the agreement in the affected countries dissipated as bankers realized that the existence of loopholes made it relatively easy to meet the evolving guidelines and even to create or refashion loopholes as needed. Loopholes can be widened in two general ways: (1) by effecting a reclassification of important assets, activities, and varieties of capital into categories that are treated more favorably or (2) by negotiating lower risk weights for particular assets and activities.

The response of large U.S. banks to the draft agreement has moved along two main paths: (1) raising new capital, primarily in the nondiluting and tax-advantaged forms of subordinated debt and convertible preferred stock (see Table 4–1), and (2) lobbying for exempting holding companies and large nonbank subsidiaries from the risk exposure base. Some small banks sought to win blanket exemptions for small-sized institutions, and in a rare show of interindustry cooperation, banks and thrifts worked together to lower the risk weighting assigned to mortgages and to eliminate

Table 4–1. Securities Issued in U.S. Capital Markets during the First 10 Months of 1988

| Date | Issuer | Amount ($ Million) | Type of Security |
|------|--------|--------------------|------------------|
| Jan. 28 | Norwest | 50 | Subordinated notes |
| April 14 | KeyCorp | 43 | Common stock |
| May 4 | First Wisconsin | 100 | Subordinated notes |
| May 9 | First Fidelity | 150 | Subordinated notes |
| May 18 | Comerica | 75 | Subordinated notes |
| July 15 | Banque Nationale | 225 | Subordinated notes |
| July 26 | Société Générale | 300 | Subordinated notes |
| Aug. 18 | Bank of Boston | 150 | Subordinated notes |
| Aug. 23 | Bank of Montreal | 150 | Subordinated notes |
| Aug. 29 | Bank of Nova Scotia | 200 | Subordinated notes |
| Aug. 29 | Toronto Dominion | 200 | Subordinated notes |
| Sept. 1 | Hibernia Corp. | 15.4 | Common stock |
| Sept. 7 | Bank of Nova Scotia | 200 | Subordinated debentures |
| Sept. 14 | One Bancorp | 40 | Subordinated notes |
| Sept. 19 | Banco de Santander | 36.6 | Common stock |
| Sept. 21 | CCNB Corp. | 9.9 | Common stock |
| Sept. 21 | Norwest | 50 | Subordinated notes |
| Sept. 22 | GBC Bancorp | 9.5 | Common stock |
| Sept. 29 | NCNB Corp. | 250 | Convertible preferred stock |
| Sept. 30 | National Australia Bank | 350 | Subordinated notes |
| Oct. 10 | Bank of Montreal | 200 | Subordinated notes |
| Oct. 25 | California First Bank | 102.6 | Common stock |
| Oct. 27 | Chemical Banking Corp. | 150 | Subordinated capital notes |

Source: Faust (1988 p. 10).

Note: These securities would qualify as Tier 1 or Tier 2 under the uniform capital requirements established in Basle, Switzerland, in July 1988.

completely the weight proposed for long-term Treasury securities.

With so many loopholes and no clear mechanism for enforcing the spirit of the agreement, the value of the capital requirement cartel so far is more symbolic than real. It allows regulators from the signatory countries to declare formally a need and ability to adapt jointly to the ongoing globalization of financial markets. Clearly, as institutional product lines fuse worldwide, the activities and strategies of financial regulators will also need to be restructured. The agreement sets up a framework within which additional and more meaningful adaptation can take place, but it is hard to believe that the agreement will significantly constrain international regulatory competition unless and until it is greatly tightened.

### Project 1992 Proposals to Unify European Banking and Securities Markets

In 1992 the transition period for the G-10's risk-based capital agreement is scheduled to end, and the agreed-upon standards are supposed to have been fully implemented. By then the European Commission also intends, as part of Project 1992, to have developed a unified banking and securities market for the European Community's 12 member countries: Belgium, Denmark, France, West Germany, Greece, Ireland, Italy, Luxembourg, the Netherlands, Portugal, Spain, and the United Kingdom. The heart of the plan is to use reciprocity to permit diversified financial services firms to operate throughout the European Community with a single license. The single license will grant powers that are as broad or "universal" as those granted by the firm's home country to banks that are based in other EC countries (Morgan Guaranty Trust 1988).

Over a more loosely defined period of time, the 17 countries that belong to the European Council (the EC countries plus the rest of Scandinavia, Switzerland, and Austria) hope to make all plastic payment cards, automated teller machines, and other payment systems completely compatible (Duffy 1988). Among other things, that could mean that small or technologically laggard card, ATM, and payment networks could develop electronic gateways into proprietary systems that have been built up at great expense over many years by pioneering rival operators. Those pioneering operators may face a painful choice between maintaining their foothold in Europe and protecting their investment in global networks. If the cost of opening their systems to European competitors exceeds the benefits of continuing to serve European markets, the pioneering operators may be induced to abandon profitable European operations to European suppliers.

Both proposals for integrating European financial markets establish a form of customs union in financial services. Trade restrictions are to be abolished among the signatory nations, and a common set of restrictions on trade between members and nonmembers is to be adopted. Any customs union creates some patterns of trade and destroys others. If only as a matter of marketing strategy, the trade creation aspects of customs unions are inevitably emphasized by their sponsors. The ostensible justification for those agreements is the liberalization of European financial markets. The feature of the twin proposals that is destructive to trade is that they have the potential to put financial services firms in non-EC countries, such as the United States and Japan, at a disadvantage. It remains to be seen whether or to what extent the goal of diverting extra-European trade to European sources is a hidden agenda item. In the meantime, U.S. and Japanese financial firms and regulators cannot afford to ignore that possibility.

The reciprocity feature of the single European license proposal threatens Japanese and U.S. firms precisely because legislators in those countries have been reluctant to grant universal financial services powers to banks and securities firms in their domestic markets. Entry into the unified European market is to be granted to subsidiaries (*not* branches) of non-EC bank and securities firms that hold a license in any EC country. Those firms will be subject to home-country supervision and restriction of activities. However, banks and securities firms outside the European Community will be guaranteed similar treatment only if their home countries' regulations grant reciprocal privileges to banks and securities firms from all EC countries. Whenever a non-EC country's regulations fail the reciprocity test, the European Commission will be authorized to bar its member states from licensing firms from that nonmember country. In that case, branch and subsidiary financial services firms from the nonconforming country that are already doing business in the European Community would be grandfathered in ways that are still being negotiated. The grandfather provisions that were discussed originally have already been liberalized. But even if grandfathered firms enjoy a blanket right to expand across the entire European Community, new entrants from the United States and Japan may face important barriers.

It would be a serious mistake to assume that either or both of the harmonization efforts are primarily intended to limit future access to European markets for U.S. and Japanese firms. Pressure for individual countries' autonomous financial policies to conform to a more progressive pan-European standard is real and deliberate. The proximate goal is the liberalization of regulations of European countries (particularly those in the South) whose present regulatory systems still constrain the international movement of capital or maintain barriers to foreign and cross-industry entry into banking, securities, and insurance activity. Seen in that light, an EC-wide banking license is a way station on what could prove to be a pan-European road to regulatory harmonization. However, like those of the risk-based capital agreement, its effects are easily exaggerated. Realistically, it reduces the amount of further adaptation that is required and provides a paradigm for future negotiation.

Nevertheless, assuming that most nonconforming countries are persuaded to liberalize their regulations, the traditional insularity with which U.S. and Japanese legislators, regulators, and financial executives have viewed their domestic regulatory systems will become increasingly costly to sustain.

## Implications for U.S. Regulatory Strategy

Regulatees can migrate to better regulators by relabeling their products, relocating their production, or adjusting their legal forms. Such migration can be thought of as a type of structural arbitrage that gives individual regulators an opportunity to enroll additional classes of regulatees. Although structural arbitrage entails nonnegligible transition costs, competition among regulators serves as a kind of social insurance. Opportunities for regulatory migration protect financial firms and their customers from the high regulatory costs that a perfected cartel or monopoly supplier might be expected to impose.

We may think of a regulator's market share as the proportionate value of the aggregate financial services business that is captured by firms that fall within its jurisdiction. Jurisdiction over multinational firms is inevitably shared as a consequence of their adapting their operations to span and integrate financial markets in different countries. It is as natural for regulators in different countries to compete for the business of those firms as it is for the firms to play the regulators of the countries in which they do business off against one another.

In recent years U.S. financial regulators have been losing market share in securities and banking to foreign regulators, particularly to the Japanese (Kane 1988). Macroeconomic events have made restraints on international financial competition more burdensome to regulatees, while technological change has made traditional restrictions easier to circumvent. As a result, those restrictions are losing force. It has become harder to shut out foreign financial services firms and to keep domestic firms from expanding their off-shore activities.

The sustained redistribution of market share to Japanese banks and securities firms is creating pressure for regulatory innovation in the world's other financial centers. Moreover, the near impossibility of exit for national regulators intensifies the pressure on those regulators to respond. Foreign governments and trade associations of "guest" firms have placed considerable political pressure on Japanese officials to improve foreign access to their domestic financial markets. For example, the U.S. Congress passed legislation in 1988 calling on the Fed not to recognize as "primary dealers" in U.S. government securities any financial institutions from countries that deny similar competitive opportunities to U.S. firms. However, eight Japanese firms already enjoy primary dealer status, and the Fed has strong bureaucratic incentives to recognize more. Additional recognitions can be rationalized on the grounds that foreign regulatory pressure and the strength of the yen have induced Japanese regulators to relax slightly restrictions on foreign entry into Japanese financial markets (e.g., into markets for bonds and commercial paper) and to begin accommodating foreign demand for Euroyen instruments.

Efforts to persuade Japanese officials to join the United States and the European countries in harmonizing capital standards foundered for a while on how to treat what the agreement calls revaluation reserves. Revaluation reserves are off-balance-sheet sources of value primarily in the form of net unrealized capital gains on securities, loans, or real estate. Such reserves are on average positive and substantial for Japanese banks (because of large amounts of unrealized gains on equity investments) and negative and substantial for large U.S. banks. Although Japanese authorities traditionally counted 70 percent of a bank's revaluation reserves as regulatory capital, American and British authorities have proved unwilling to acknowledge the relevance of market value measures of bank capital. Such an acknowledgment would threaten in the long run to narrow those authorities' capacity to hide evidence of cumulative weakness in their regulatory performance. Western officials' comical claim that the relatively low *book value* of Japanese banks' capital position gives them an advantage in competing with American banks for loan, guarantee, and deposit business shows that legislators and regulators tend to confuse even themselves by their accounting smoke and mirrors.

The advantage of Japanese banks and securities firms lies in their being strongly capitalized on a market value basis (Kane 1988). Market values are the relevant measures of a bank's ability to absorb losses and/or to withstand a depositor run. Moreover, there is no reason to believe that hidden reserves are more vulnerable to market fluctuations than are other sources of bank capital. Concern about asset volatility should apply to all elements of an institution's portfolio. Although in measuring a client's financial strength, regulators might scale down the market value of volatile items, it makes no sense for regulators to assign a zero weight to hidden reserves.

## Conclusion

U.S. officials assume that structural arbitrage can be contained by negotiating a formal harmonization of individual countries' approaches to financial regulation. This paper's industrial-organization perspective indicates why such regulatory agreements do not necessarily promote the common good. It also makes it clear that the difficulty of establishing durable patterns of international regulatory cooperation reflects difficulties inherent in forming and maintaining a worldwide cartel to control any product or service. Moreover, in the long run—no matter what the sponsors of a regulatory cartel may think they can accomplish by negotiation— market forces will reshape the result.

Improvements in regulatory or tax burdens that structural arbitrage attains for multinational and multipurpose financial firms are often generated by shifting real costs to underinformed or lethargic taxpayers. The most important of those hidden costs are unintended subsidies that flow from the improper pricing of explicit and implicit government and international financial guarantees. Concealing those subsidies from taxpayers makes their long-run effects destabilizing. Systematic governmental disinformation policies make it hard for taxpayers to fill the disciplinary role that stockholders and creditors play in a private firm. As a result, inefficient regulators can and do perversely mine the policy crises they cause for new powers and larger budgets.

Increased accountability on the part of the financial regulators of all countries is the missing ingredient in current efforts at financial harmonization. It is a mistake for society to let regulators be judged merely by their rhetorically noble ostensible intentions. Of course, we should not suppose that improving the quality of information about financial regulatory performance would put an end to regulatory subsidies, but economic theory does promise that selective subsidies can be constrained by making their production more costly to their beneficiaries.

The international regulatory agreements examined in this paper suggest that Western financial services firms and regulators are counting on the risk-based capital agreement and increased foreign entry into Japanese financial markets to slow future penetration of international financial markets by Japanese banks and securities firms. If so, they have much to learn about both what makes Japanese banks tough competitors and how an institution's capital ought to be valued.

## Notes

1. This section draws extensively on Kane (1988).

2. Actually, 12 countries were represented on the Committee on Banking Regulations and Supervisory Practices that developed the agreement: Belgium, Canada, France, West Germany, Italy, Japan, Luxembourg, the Netherlands, Sweden, Switzerland, the United Kingdom, and the United States (Friesen 1988).

## References

Baumol, William, Panzar, John C., and Willig, Robert. 1986. "On the Theory of Contestable Markets." In *New Developments in the Theory of Industrial Structure*, edited by G. F. Matthewson and Joseph E. Stiglitz. Cambridge, Mass: MIT Press, pp. 339–72.

Duffy, John J. 1988. "17-Nation Pact Unifies Payment Systems." *American Banker*, May 25, pp. 1, 22, 23.

Faust, Bart. 1988. "Bank, Thrift Issues Slowed in October." *American Banker*, November 15, pp. 3, 8, 10.

Friesen, Connie M. 1988. "Capital Guidelines and Global Markets." *Review of Financial Services Regulation* 4 (July): 123–31.

Giddy, Ian H. 1984. "Domestic Regulation versus International Competition in Banking." *Kredit und Kapital* 8, pp. 195–209.

Kane, Edward J. 1988. "How Market Forces Influence the Structure of Financial Regulation." In *Restructuring the Financial System*, edited by William Haraf and Rose Marie Kushmeider. Washington D.C.: American Enterprise Institute, pp. 343–82.

Morgan Guaranty Trust Company. 1988. "Financial Markets in Europe: Toward 1992." *World Financial Markets*, September 9, pp. 1–15.

Niskanen, William. 1971. *Bureaucracy and Representative Government*. Chicago: Aldine.

Pearce, David W., ed. 1986. *The MIT Dictionary of Modern Economics*. 3d ed. Cambridge, Mass.: MIT Press.

Scott, Kenneth E. 1977. "The Dual Banking System: A Model of Competition in Regulation." *Stanford Law Review* 30, pp. 1–50.

Stigler, George. 1971. "The Theory of Economic Regulation." *Bell Journal of Economics* 2 (Spring): 113–21.

# COMMENT ON INTERNATIONAL COORDINATION OF REGULATION

Michael C. Keeley

The papers in this volume by Michael Laub and Edward Kane discuss the merits of international coordination of bank regulation. They focus on the recent international agreement on risk-based capital and on the proposed financial integration of the European Community in 1992.

Laub argues that the lack of uniformity in the deposit insurance systems and in other financial regulatory features of the various countries makes it somewhat pointless to try to coordinate capital regulation. Instead, Laub supports national financial regulation and corresponding national responsibility for domestic financial stability and monetary policy.

Kane compares international regulatory coordination with the formation of cartels. The analysis offers an interesting perspective; however, I am unsure where Kane really stands on recent coordination attempts. On the

The author is a vice president of Cornerstone Research. This paper was prepared while the author was a research officer at the Federal Reserve Bank of San Francisco. The views expressed herein are those of the author and do not necessarily reflect the views of Cornerstone Research, the Federal Reserve Bank of San Francisco, or the Board of Governors of the Federal Reserve System.

one hand, he argues that an international regulatory cartel is undesirable because it would suppress regulatory competition to the detriment of the regulated entities and consumers, just as private cartels can harm social welfare. On the other hand, he claims that regulatory cartels face the same problems of cheating that private cartels face and that they are therefore unlikely to be successful. Instead, market forces will ultimately shape financial markets.

I think that there is considerable merit to certain aspects of each of those views. Before turning to the details of the papers, however, I would like to step back and consider the purposes of bank regulation in general. Bank regulation is a difficult topic to address. We lack a consensus on the ideal type of bank and financial regulation for the United States, and designing an international set of coordinated regulations is surely much more difficult. For the United States, we have proposals as diverse as imposing risk-based deposit insurance premiums or risk-based capital requirements; eliminating or scaling back deposit insurance; requiring market value accounting, closer monitoring of bank capital, and prompt market value closure rules; and reviving Henry Simons's and Milton Friedman's proposals for so-called narrow banking.

## The Purpose of Bank Regulation

Before attempting to decide how much cooperation is needed in international bank regulation, it is necessary to try to spell out the fundamental purpose of such regulation. Laub offers the conventional argument that banks are uniquely prone to runs that may spread and cause even solvent institutions to fail. Thus, the failure of a few banks can lead to a general panic, and bank regulation is required to protect the industry from the threat of collapse by preventing runs from starting. That traditional rationale for bank regulation warrants further consideration.

First, several studies have argued that the importance of contagion effects has been overemphasized [for example, see Gorton (1988) and Kaufman (1985)]. Many of those studies note that the empirical evidence in support of contagion is weak. Second, if contagion due to lack of reliable information is the key rationale for bank regulation, why not just require that bank authorities or even private bond-rating firms make information publicly available to prevent contagion? Why institute deposit insurance and the cumbersome regulatory apparatus that it entails?[1]

Some would therefore argue that deposit insurance is unnecessary and that without federal deposit insurance only a minimal amount of bank regulation would be needed. Perhaps some form of self-regulation would suffice.

I cannot provide a definitive answer about the presence or absence of serious contagion effects, nor can I determine fully whether bank regulation is needed. But surely those issues are key to the reform of bank regulation in general and to the determination of the desirability of international coordination in particular.

For example, suppose the failure of one bank does impose externalities on other banks, some of which are located in other countries, by increasing the likelihood of runs on them or of their failure, or both. It seems unlikely that domestic regulation would necessarily lead to the complete internalization of such externalities. Presumably, the increasingly interrelated nature of the world's financial system, which is identified and emphasized by both authors, would be reason enough to be concerned that a domestic panic might spread to other countries. If so, that would be an important argument in support of international coordination, although the question raised by Kane of whether such coordination would break down under market forces would remain.

On the other hand, if runs on individual institutions do not have serious contagion effects, there would seem to be little need for international regulation.[2] As Laub proposes, each country could decide how best to prevent domestic bank runs. Perhaps a competitive regulatory system, such as that envisioned by Kane, would work.

My purpose is not to support one of those views over the other but to argue that it is difficult to assess the merits of international regulatory coordination without first deciding whether there are international externalities involved in bank runs. Therefore, I maintain that Laub's conclusions are not consistent with his assumptions. Kane's conclusions are more difficult to judge because his paper fails to delineate where he stands on the question of contagion effects.

In a sense, the issue of international coordination is very similar to the issue of dual banking in the United States. Both Laub and Kane discuss the merits and drawbacks of regulatory competition, but even that issue revolves crucially around whether a run on one bank imposes externalities on others. If it does, it is hard for either private market competition or regulatory competition to force internalization of the resulting externalities. Although one can point to many benefits of the dual banking system, such as forcing regulators over time to eliminate many inefficient regulations that are apparently unrelated to safety and soundness, regulatory competition also has the potential to destabilize the banking system and bankrupt the deposit insurance agencies. The expansion of thrift powers by state chartering agencies without concern for the potential increase in the federal deposit insurance system's risk exposure is an example.

Although I believe that regulators' actions, just like those of academics and private businessmen, are subject to the forces of competition, it appears that political competition, not market competition, is the main force disciplining regulators. If market competition could do the job, there would be no need for government regulation in the first place. If any regulation were needed, self-regulation would probably be sufficient. In some sense, that may be the argument Kane is making.

## Risk-Based Capital

Let me turn now to the question of whether a uniform international system of risk-based capital regulation is desirable. The most common rationale for such a system is that it will somehow level the playing field for banks that operate internationally. I have my doubts about that argument.

First, Modigliani and Miller (1958) demonstrated that a firm's capital structure is irrelevant, absent distortions such as taxes, agency costs, bankruptcy costs, and in the case of banking, deposit insurance. Some of those distortions, especially deposit insurance, may be important; their presence and form will influence the optimal capital structure of banks. Thus, there would seem to be little point in equalizing capital regulations internationally unless the other potentially distorting forces are also equalized. Perhaps that is the point Laub is trying to make.

For example, little would be gained by equalizing capital regulations in two countries if their deposit insurance systems had very different coverage or other features. Similarly, because a country's tax policy affects the relative costs of capital and deposits, equalizing capital requirements across borders without equalizing tax structures will fail to place internationally competitive banks from different countries on an equal footing. Banks from countries that treat equity more favorably than debt will be able to raise additional capital at less cost than banks from countries, such as the United States, that favor debt over equity. Similarly, if two countries with comparable deposit insurance systems allow banks very different asset powers but require identical capital levels, the banks in the country with the more restrictive asset powers will be at a competitive disadvantage.

It is not clear, however, how important those distortions are. In the United States at least, nonbanking financial firms with different capital structures seem to be able to compete, both with each other and to a certain extent with banks, and even banking organizations with different capital structures can and do compete with each other. A more compelling justification of the international coordination of capital standards may be that it is intended to limit intercountry regulatory competition that could lead to reduced capital standards and increased deposit insurance subsidies. Thus far no trend in that direction is apparent, but Kane seems to imply that one could develop.

Finally, both Kane and Laub offer some well deserved criticism of the details of the risk-based capital proposal: it relies on historical book values rather than market-based accounting to measure capital, it focuses on individual asset risk weights rather than measuring overall portfolio risk, and it entirely neglects interest rate risk. Nevertheless, the proposal is a step in the right direction, especially compared with the status quo. To dwell on the accord's shortcomings is to miss several important points that might be desirable for the United States alone to implement.

First, the standards are generally more stringent than are current U.S. standards and thus would lead to higher capitalization ratios, especially for large money center banks. More capital is desirable for two reasons: it provides a greater cushion for any decline in an institution's asset value, and more capital relative to assets reduces the incentive for institutions to increase their asset risk [see Keeley (1990) and Furlong and Keeley (1989)]. Thus, more stringent capital standards should reduce the risk exposure of the deposit insurance funds.

Second, the standards establish the *principle* of requiring that an institution's capital reflect its risk. In keeping with that principle, the accord explicitly recognizes that off-balance-sheet activities can impose risks on banks that pursue them and on the deposit insurance system. Therefore, those activities should be subject to capital requirements that are equivalent to those for on-balance-sheet items that represent similar risks.

Finally, the standards are not considered final or immutable. All parties wish to improve the risk-based system over time. Indeed, work is currently proceeding on incorporating interest rate risk into the standards.

## 1992 European Financial Integration

Both Kane and Laub also touch on the proposed 1992 integration of European banking. As Laub describes the proposal, it sounds very much like our dual banking system multiplied many times over. That would really introduce competition among regulators!

Laub notes that competition among different European countries' banking systems after 1992 may result in eventual domination by the universal banking systems of West Germany and Switzerland. I find it hard to see why that would be such a bad thing. However, I do agree with Kane and Laub that the potential exclusion of non-European banks, particularly U.S. and Japanese banks, from the post-1992 European market is a probable and undesirable consequence.

## Corporate Separateness

Finally, although corporate separateness is usually proposed as a means of insulating banks from their domestic nonbank affiliates, Laub emphasizes, correctly I think, that it would be a key component of his proposed system of international regulatory standards because, under his proposal, foreign affiliates might be subjected to very different regulations than are domestic banks.

However, it seems to me that there is something of a logical contradiction in relying on corporate separateness alone to insulate domestic banks and the domestic deposit insurance fund from the possibly riskier activities of those banks' foreign affiliates. First, I question whether it is possible to achieve meaningful corporate separation without losing most of the advantages of affiliation. If the activities of a bank's affiliates are truly separated from the bank both financially and managerially, the affiliate essentially becomes a passive investment. It is hard to see why, in such a case, there would be any advantages or synergies to combining foreign and domestic banking activities within a single organization in the first place.

Second, reliance on corporate separateness may lull us into a false sense of security about the insulation of a bank from the risks of its affiliates. There are many ways organizations can exchange resources and share risk. The means will be found to breach the fire wall, either within the letter of the law or, if necessary, illegally, if the incentives are strong enough.

Personally, I favor more stringent market-based capital regulation that would include both more frequent monitoring and a strictly enforced market value capital closure rule. Under such a system, we could be more certain that the risks of banking organizations were borne by their capital holders, not by the deposit insurance system. As a result, banks would have much stronger incentives to control their own risk taking. Moreover, less restrictive fire walls could be used so that more of the advantages or synergies of combining domestic and foreign banking activities, as well as nontraditional banking activities, could be realized.

## Notes

1. Another rationale for preventing bank runs comes from an interesting article by Diamond and Dybvig (1983). In their model, even runs on an individual bank impose social costs because runs disrupt credit intermediation and real output. Thus, deposit insurance can increase social welfare by preventing all bank runs.

2. That would be true even if it could be demonstrated that noncontagious runs result in a greater overall reduction of social welfare than they do under a system that includes federal deposit insurance.

## References

Diamond, Douglas W., and Dybvig, Philip H. 1983. "Bank Runs, Deposit Insurance and Liquidity." *Journal of Political Economy* 91, no. 3, pp. 401–19.

Furlong, Frederick T., and Keeley, Michael C. 1989. "Capital Regulation and Bank Risk-Taking: A Note." *Journal of Banking and Finance* 13, pp. 883–91.

Gorton, Gary. 1988. "Banking Panics and Business Cycles." *Oxford Economic Papers* 40, pp. 751–81.

Kaufman, George G. 1985. "Implications of Large Bank Problems and Insolvencies for the Banking System and Economic Policy." Working Paper SM-85-3. Federal Reserve Bank of Chicago.

Keeley, Michael C. 1990. "Deposit Insurance, Risk and Market Power in Banking." *American Economic Review* 80, no. 5 (December): 1183–1200.

Modigliani, Franco, and Miller, Merton. 1958. "The Cost of Capital, Corporation Finance and the Theory of Investment." *American Economic Review* 48, no. 3 (June): 261–97.

# III BANK INSULATION

# 5 CAN BANKS BE INSULATED FROM NONBANK AFFILIATES?

James L. Pierce

Congress, bank regulators, and conference participants have spent a great deal of time and attention on the issue of insulating banks within their holding companies. Interest in that rather arcane topic is increasing because the bank insulation issue has become intertwined with the debate over allowing banking organizations to exercise additional powers such as offering a full line of securities or insurance services.

There is a growing awareness that banking organizations must be allowed to provide additional financial services if they are to compete and prosper in the modern, highly integrated financial environment.[1] Banking organizations are displaying increasing instability and frequent lackluster performance largely because they are prevented from providing many financial services that are in high demand. Unable to adapt to the changing environment by offering additional services, the banking industry has seen securities markets and nonbank financial conglomerates draw away many of its prized customers. Much of the cream has been skimmed off, and

The author is a professor of economics at the University of California at Berkeley.

bankers have had only low-fat milk as a replacement. The results are all too visible: a rising tide of failures, near failures, and federal bailouts.

The issues of bank insulation and new powers have been combined because there is concern that any substantial new powers for banks qua banks would increase risks to the deposit insurance fund to unacceptable levels. Accordingly, it has been proposed that bank holding companies, but not banks, be allowed to engage in new activities only if banks can be insulated from any potential losses associated with those activities. This paper examines insulation and new powers for banking organizations as two logically separate issues, each of which should be addressed on its own. Once that has been done, the issues are joined.

## Insulation

### Is Insulation Feasible?

In assessing the feasibility of insulating banks from the nonbank elements of their holding companies, one must ask, insulated from what? The standard answer is that banks should be insulated from losses suffered by nonbank affiliates that could weaken or endanger the bank. That sort of insulation is certainly feasible and, to the extent the law is enforced, already exists to a large degree.

Without defining "bank," at this point it can be said that a corporate organization called a bank can be insulated from losses incurred by other corporate organizations with which it is affiliated within a holding company. That issue has been put to rest in a recent paper by Chase, Laub and Company (1987) on which I rely for background.

**The Current Status of Insulation.**   Considerable insulation exists under current law and regulation. Section 23A of the Federal Reserve Act[2] limits the loans, credit guarantees, and asset purchases of a bank to no more than 10 percent of its capital and surplus for any given nonbank affiliate, and to no more than 20 percent for all nonbank affiliates combined. Furthermore, the loans must be secured by collateral, typically worth more than 100 percent of the loan. Section 23B of the Federal Reserve Act requires that loans, fees, and other business transactions between a bank and its nonbank affiliates be at arm's length. That requirement extends to activities that the holding company sponsors or advises such as real estate investment trusts. In addition to legal restrictions, bank regulators have authority to limit dividends paid by a bank to its holding company and to limit other activities involving contacts with its holding company affiliates that might threaten the bank's safety and soundness.

In a nutshell, current restrictions are quite stringent. If existing laws and regulations are enforced, it is difficult for banking organizations to use transactions between a bank and its nonbank affiliates (including the parent company) in a manner that could seriously weaken the bank.

**Improving Insulation.** Current procedures for insulating banks should be improved, however, and it would be relatively easy to tighten them. All transactions between a bank and its nonbank affiliates would not have to be eliminated; loopholes could be closed and some ambiguities cleared up. For example, daylight overdrafts granted by a bank to its nonbank affiliates in the course of executing electronic payment transactions currently are not included in the credit limits under Section 23A. A company that does not have sufficient funds in its bank account at the time it wants to make an electronic payment can receive an overdraft (loan) from its bank. The overdraft is eliminated when the company collects funds later in the same day. A company experiencing financial difficulties might default on the overdraft, however, and thereby subject the bank to losses. Banks can be insulated against losses on daylight overdrafts extended to nonbank affiliates by requiring that those overdrafts be included in the definition of credit extended to nonbank affiliates under Section 23A.[3]

As another example, the Garn–St Germain Act of 1982 amended the Federal Reserve Act to remove most of the restrictions on transactions between a bank and its subsidiaries, apparently on the premise that a bank's subsidiaries are an integral part of the parent bank. Be that as it may, that provision weakens bank insulation directly by exposing the parent bank to losses sustained by its subsidiaries. It also has the indirect effect of encouraging bank holding companies to shift activities from nonbank affiliates to subsidiaries of their bank or banks. Such shifts are possible because there is often little that nonbank affiliates can do that banks or their subsidiaries are not also allowed to do. (Additional potential incentives for the shifts are discussed later.) Bank insulation can be improved by rescinding the 1982 amendments to the Federal Reserve Act.

As a final example of how insulation can be improved, Congress, in the Competitive Equality Banking Act of 1987, prohibited banks from representing in any way that they are responsible for the obligations of their nonbank affiliates. That is an indirect, backhanded way to improve insulation. The situation would be improved if nonbank affiliates, including parent companies, were required to make prominent and clear declarations in debt instruments (including commercial paper) and prospectuses that their debt is not an obligation of a bank and is not backed by federal deposit insurance. That change is important because, in the absence of an explicit disclaimer, there is some chance that creditors of nonbank affiliates or of the parent company could "pierce the corporate veil" by arguing that they thought the obligations they bought were backed by the bank. Should such efforts prove successful, a bank would not be insulated. That potential problem is easy to avoid.

**If Insulation Is Feasible, Why the Concern?**    Legal and regulatory insulation of banks from the misfortunes of their nonbank affiliates is feasible. Since insulation is already quite thick and can be improved easily, why are people so interested in bank insulation? The answer is less than clear, but there seem to be two areas of concern.

First, some reformers assert that there will be room for abuse as long as there is *any* contact between banks and their nonbank affiliates. They want to eliminate all temptation to expose banks to losses incurred by their nonbank affiliates by prohibiting all transactions and all contact between a bank and its nonbank affiliates. That approach would guarantee insulation, but it is neither necessary nor desirable. As long as transactions are limited in amount and conducted at arm's length, as is the case under current law, it is highly unlikely that the failure of an affiliate could bring down a bank. That possibility would be reduced further still if existing restrictions were tightened as suggested. It is difficult to see why the risk of loss as the result of dealings with affiliates should be driven to zero. Prohibiting transactions and other contact would provide insulation all right, but at the cost of needlessly interfering with business decisions.

Banks confront risk in virtually all of their activities. The purpose of bank regulation is to limit and control risk, not to eliminate it. Furthermore, if banks are deprived of contact with their affiliates—sharing skilled personnel, data bases, and physical capital—banking organizations lose the economies of scale and scope that make holding company operations attractive in the first place. To cut off such sharing in a heavy-handed effort to achieve insulation would be to throw the baby out with the bath water. The purpose of insulation should be to protect a bank from failing or from suffering large losses should its affiliates experience difficulties, not to cut off all contact.

The second area of concern about bank insulation is more fundamental and more subtle because it involves the attitudes and policies of a bank regulator rather than the law. The Federal Reserve Board, which is responsible for regulating bank holding companies, is unwilling to embrace the principle of bank insulation as a regulatory tool. In both its statements and its policies, the Fed has taken the position that insulation is impossible.

Before criticizing the Federal Reserve, fairness requires that its policies be put in context. The Fed's policies concerning bank holding companies evolved during a period when bank insulation made little sense. The rapid growth of bank holding companies in the 1960s and 1970s was the product of attempts by banks to circumvent arbitrary regulations. The holding company format allowed banks to do banking by another name. For example, branching restrictions in states like Texas could be circumvented by operating several banks within a holding company. Similarly, bank holding companies could get around restrictions on interstate branching, which prohibited banks from engaging in business and consumer lending across state lines, by operating loan production facilities, consumer finance companies, and mortgage-banking firms. A portion of the funds used to support those activities came from negotiable certificates of deposit and similar instruments issued by banks both nationwide and around the world—to the extent such transactions were consistent with Section 23A of the Federal Reserve Act—but funds were raised primarily through debt instruments issued by the nonbank affiliates themselves. Given those circumstances, the Federal Reserve viewed the debt issued by nonbank affiliates as bank liabilities under another name. That prompted the Fed to, among other things, be concerned about the "double leverage" provided by holding company debt.[4] Finally, many banks formed holding companies in the late 1960s as a means of circumventing regulation of the interest rates that banks could pay on their negotiable CDs and other domestic liabilities. Obligations of the parent company and of nonbank affiliates were not bank deposits and, therefore, not subject to interest rate ceilings. Once again, it was natural to view those obligations as bank liabilities in disguise.

Thus, bank holding companies were initially formed by banks as vehicles for doing banking. When laws and regulations prevented the conduct of certain types of business within a bank, the business was done through the holding company, but it remained banking. In that environment the Federal Reserve naturally viewed bank holding companies as banks with another name. In both a management and an economic sense, there really was no separation between banks and other elements of their holding companies, so it was natural for the Fed to view its regulatory duties as carrying over to nonbank elements of holding companies.

The Federal Reserve did not make those inferences all on its own. The Bank Holding Company Act essentially restricts the activities of bank holding companies to those that are permitted banks themselves. In particular, bank holding companies are to engage only in activities that are "closely related" to or "coincident" with banking. Thus, the law itself views the activities of nonbank affiliates as banking by another name. Both the Federal Reserve and Congress implicitly took the position that there was only a corporate veil separating banks from other elements of their holding companies.

As the Federal Reserve's interpretation of permissible activities has broadened, as nonbank affiliates have grown larger, and as nonbank affiliates have taken on lives of their own distinct from those of affiliated banks, the issue of bank insulation has become increasingly important. The Fed has elected to respond by increasing its doses of the same old medicine. Supervision of the activities of nonbank affiliates has been increased; reporting requirements have been raised; and minimum capital standards for holding companies, as distinct from subsidiary banks, have been imposed. In short, the Fed has elected to continue to regulate bank holding companies as if they were banks.

The Federal Reserve has offered two justifications for its approach. First, it asserts that a bank holding company is to be a "source of strength" for its subsidiary bank or banks. The meaning of that term is not totally clear, but it seems to imply one-sided insulation. The bank is largely insulated by law and regulation from misfortunes suffered by other elements of the holding company, but those elements are not insulated from the misfortunes of their affiliated bank or banks. The resources of the nonbank parts of a holding company are to be available to the bank subsidiary during periods of adversity, but not vice versa. To ensure that financial resources are available should the bank need them, the Fed regulates and supervises bank holding companies and imposes minimum capital requirements on them. (The law requires minimum capital standards only for banks, not for holding companies.) The policies of the Federal Reserve undermine much of the separation that otherwise would exist between banks and their holding companies. Those policies could create substantial problems when bank holding companies are granted new powers. For example, the Federal Reserve could look to securities subsidiaries of a holding company to act as a source of strength to affiliated banks, but the banks presumably would be prohibited from providing financial resources to securities subsidiaries. That issue is discussed in more detail later.

The second way in which the Federal Reserve rejects insulation is through its concern about the consequences for a bank if one of its affiliates should encounter difficulties or fail. The Fed is concerned that financial difficulties experienced by a nonbank affiliate could raise doubts among creditors about the safety of the affiliated bank. Should creditors lose confidence, the bank's borrowing costs would rise, at a minimum, and it is possible that the bank would not be able to roll over its maturing negotiable CDs and similar obligations. If that happened, the bank could experience major liquidity strains. The Fed is apparently worried that if the liquidity crunch were large enough, an otherwise solvent bank could be forced into insolvency by massive asset sales at depressed prices.

It is difficult to make sense of that argument. The solvent but liquidity-strained bank could probably raise sufficient money in the interbank market, obviating the need to sell illiquid assets. But suppose it could not. The Federal Reserve's discount window exists precisely to handle that kind of problem. The bank would have to borrow from the Fed for a while until it was able to regain the confidence of its creditors. Then the bank could repay its loans from the central bank. Such temporary use of the discount window hardly constitutes a crisis, and it helps insulate the bank from the misfortunes of its nonbank affiliates. The Federal Reserve's position might be justified if there were no discount window, but it seems indefensible in reality.

The Federal Reserve is also concerned about bankers' responses if troubles in a nonbank affiliate shake bank creditors' confidence. The Fed is apparently convinced that, to protect itself, a bank would be forced to provide whatever assistance was needed by a troubled nonbank affiliate to protect the bank's good name; to do otherwise would threaten the bank. Assertion of such a response has been made eloquently by Walter Wriston (1981, pp. 589–90), the former head of Citicorp, the nation's largest bank holding company:

> It is inconceivable that any major bank would walk away from any subsidiary of its holding company. If your name is on the door, all of your capital funds are going to be behind it in the real world. Lawyers can say you have separation, but the marketplace is persuasive, and it would not see it that way.

Wriston seems to be suggesting that a bank would be forced to make funds available to protect a nonbank affiliate even if in so doing the bank violated Sections 23A and 23B of the Federal Reserve Act.

Statements like Wriston's apparently have led the Federal Reserve to conclude that the prospect of the failure of a nonbank affiliate so threatens the good name of an affiliated bank that the bank would take desperate measures to protect the affiliate. It is difficult to evaluate the importance of protecting a bank's good name, but there is more involved. If major bank holding companies can convince creditors of their nonbank affiliates or parent company that the affiliated bank will come to the rescue of nonbank affiliates, borrowing costs for the nonbank affiliates will be reduced. Through their overzealous application of the federal safety net to protect large banks, the bank regulators guarantee those banks against failure. Thus, a bank claims that it will protect its nonbank affiliates, and the federal government protects the bank. In effect, banks in a holding company try to convince creditors of nonbank affiliates that the federal safety net extends indirectly to them. To the extent banks are successful in those efforts, their nonbank affiliates and parent companies can borrow at lower interest rates.

The conclusion one should reach is not that effective insulation of banks is impossible, as the Fed apparently believes, but that the laws preventing bailouts of nonbank subsidiaries by banks should be enforced. It also is quite possible that the penalties for breaking the law are not sufficiently harsh. (It is remarkable that the Federal Reserve has not asked Congress for harsher penalties.) The current penalty for violating Section 23A, for example, is $1,000 per day. That is hardly a deterrent for major bank holding companies. Insulation of banks could be enhanced if penalties for violations of current laws were more severe. It is highly unlikely, for example, that bank officers would knowingly violate restrictions on transactions between banks and nonbank affiliates if they faced a jail sentence for the violation.

In summary, the Federal Reserve's position on the feasibility of insulating banks appears to be untenable. It is possible to achieve the degree of insulation necessary to effectively protect a bank from being seriously weakened or failing as a consequence of adversity experienced by its nonbank affiliates. The federal safety net need not and should not be extended to nonbank affiliates.[5]

### Is Insulation Desirable?

Although effective insulation is feasible, it has not been established that insulation is necessarily desirable. Resolution of that issue is less straightforward than it may at first appear.

Effective bank insulation cuts two ways. It shields a bank from losses suffered by nonbank affiliates, but it also deprives a bank of profits earned by its nonbank affiliates. A bank holding company may choose to direct some of the profits from nonbank units to a bank, but it is not required to do so.[6] There is little reason to believe that those profits will be shared with an affiliated bank except to the extent necessary to help keep the bank within the minimum capital guidelines established by regulation. The two-sided nature of insulation needs to be kept in mind when assessing the implications of new powers for banking organizations. If the new activities are housed in nonbank affiliates, bank holding companies will gain, but insulated banks will not. Banks will still have to rely on the same activities as before. About all a bank stands to gain is the possibility of acquiring new banking business that is attracted because the bank is affiliated with a holding company that provides a wide variety of services. Any potential gain is likely to be more than offset, however, by losses to bank income caused by shifts of currently allowable securities and insurance activities from banks and bank subsidiaries to nonbank securities and insurance affiliates.[7]

It is unfortunate that discussions of new powers for banking organizations have focused almost exclusively on shielding banks from risk; the profit potential created by expanded bank powers should be considered as well. There is little in the proposals to house new powers in nonbank affiliates of holding companies that will make banks more profitable and stable or less prone to failure. Stockholders of bank holding companies will benefit, but not banks. Those concerned about the profitability of banks, including the Federal Deposit Insurance Corporation, should think twice before recommending that new activities be housed in separate nonbank affiliates.

My comments should not be interpreted as a criticism of allowing new powers for banking organizations or of housing new activities in nonbank affiliates; they are not. The comments are made to illustrate that the bank insulation issue is complex. To address it properly requires discussion of what insulation does and does not accomplish. More fundamentally, to make progress on the issue, it is necessary to determine what a "bank" is; that is, we must identify the services that are so essential that they should be insulated from other financial services activities.

**Insulation in the Absence of Government Regulation and Protection.** It is convenient to begin the discussion of the desirability of bank insulation with a brief analysis of corporate substructures in general. Consider a world in which there is no government insurance, protection, or regulation of banks. In that situation, the division of activities among various components of a banking (financial services) organization would be a matter of management choice. There are benefits and costs associated with dividing activities among a number of separate corporations, and there are benefits and costs associated with housing everything within a single corporation.

One advantage of operating several separate corporations within a holding company structure is the benefit of limited liability. As long as each corporation has its own board of directors, has a different name, and observes other niceties required for corporate separateness,[8] its creditors and others have a claim only on the specific corporation to which they lend or with which they have other dealings. Thus, corporate separateness allows each corporation to be insulated from the fortunes of every other corporation. There may be good business reasons for affiliated firms' coming to the assistance of a sister firm in difficulty (including protecting the reputations of the holding company and financially stronger affiliates), but the decision is made by management. Thus, operating a number of separate corporations limits the risk to each while retaining the ability to engage in intra-holding-company bailouts when economic considerations justify doing so.[9]

Operating separate corporations also makes it easier to deal with clashes of different corporate cultures and pay standards for personnel. For example, the corporate culture of conventional banking tends to be more conservative than that of many securities activities, and bank employees tend to earn less income. It may be easier to deal with those differences by conducting each activity in a separate corporation than by trying to achieve compatibility within a single organization.

There are also costs associated with operating a number of separate corporations, however. Communication and coordination may become difficult, and economies of scale and scope may be reduced substantially. It is more difficult to exploit synergies when activities are decentralized.

The benefits and costs of operating a single corporation are the opposite of those of the multicorporate form. It is easier to exploit synergies and to solve communication and coordination problems. On the negative side, dealing with clashes of culture and different pay scales is more difficult. Finally, with all operations under one corporate roof, the full advantages of limited liability cannot be exploited.

In the absence of government insurance, protection, and regulation, the question of how an organization balances the benefits and costs of different corporate structures requires an important management decision. That decision determines, among other things, the degree of insulation that any particular set of activities has from others. There is no reason to believe that government officials would have anything useful to contribute to that decision.

**The Effects of Regulation and Protection on Corporate Structures.** The nature of the game is fundamentally changed, however, when certain activities are subject to government regulation and protection while others are not. Suppose there are two sets of activities housed within a bank holding company. The first set of activities is supported by liabilities that are insured and guaranteed by the government, and the conduct of those activities is regulated by the government in an effort to control risk taking. That set of activities is conducted by what we shall call a bank. The other set of activities is supported by liabilities that receive no government insurance or protection and are not regulated, even though some of the unregulated, uninsured activities may be the same as those conducted within the bank. Nonbank subsidiaries conduct those activities. Finally, suppose that the bank part of the holding company is effectively insulated from the affairs of its nonbank affiliates.

Such a regulatory environment will affect the choices management makes about which activities are conducted by the bank and which are carried out by the nonbank. With the government backing only the bank's liabilities, the cost of borrowing is lower for the bank than for the nonbank, which creates an incentive to house activities involving position taking (i.e., issuing liabilities to fund asset holdings) within the bank. That involves not only conventional lending but also underwriting, securitization, and providing credit backstops such as standby letters of credit. The position taking involved in the latter activities may be short term or provisional, but the ability to issue low-cost liabilities to support them is still important. Other activities involving services, such as data processing and discount brokerage, do not involve position taking so there is reason to conduct them in the unregulated nonbank part of the holding company.

Of course the division of activities between the bank and nonbank parts of a holding company depends not only on whether borrowed funds are used to finance the activity or asset but also on the nature and degree of regulation of banking activities. Here we are not talking about regulations designed to achieve insulation of the bank but of regulation of types and degrees of lending, capital requirements, and other efforts to limit the risk of the bank's activities. The more restrictive and onerous the regulations, the greater the incentive to shift activities to the nonbank. That incentive is particularly strong for activities that are not very risky and rely on short-term credit for support. In those cases the borrowing costs for the nonbank will not significantly exceed those for the bank. Various forms of investment banking fall in that category. The most risky activities will tend to remain in the bank.

Each holding company will factor in the tradeoff between reduced borrowing costs and increased regulation in determining how it divides activities between its bank and nonbank subsidiaries. The activities that are housed within the bank will be determined largely by that tradeoff. Under the conditions outlined, what constitutes a bank will be determined endogenously in response to the incentives to issue protected liabilities on the one hand and the desire to avoid onerous regulation on the other. There is no archetype called a bank; a bank is an institution that emerges in response to government subsidies and restrictions. A different configuration would evolve if the government incentives and penalties were changed.

**Holding Companies in Real Life.**  Of course, bank holding companies do not operate in the ideal world described above. The nonbank parts of holding companies are also regulated. Perhaps the regulation is not as restrictive, but the differences are relatively slight. In large part, nonbank components of holding companies are regulated as though they were banks (e.g., they are subject to risk-based capital requirements). Activities are conducted in nonbank components largely to avoid clashes of corporate culture and to circumvent branching restrictions.

Fortunately, the regulators have recently reversed the precedent established in 1984 by the Continental Illinois fiasco, in which the FDIC bailed out the holding company along with the bank. Now apparently the creditors of the nonbank parts of holding companies are at risk. When First Oklahoma Bancorp and Republic BankCorp collapsed in 1986 and 1988, respectively, their holding company creditors did sustain losses. The FDIC protected all the creditors of the affiliated banks but not the creditors of the parent companies or of nonbank affiliates. That surely was a step in the right direction because it reversed the regulators' tendency to protect everything in sight. But bank holding companies have, predictably, been attempting to undo the effects. Faced with the higher borrowing costs paid by nonbank subsidiaries because of the greater risk faced by their creditors, holding companies have been induced to shift activities from nonbank affiliates either directly to their banks or to subsidiaries of their banks. Such shifting is likely to intensify as branching restrictions continue to crumble. With nonbank affiliates regulated much like banks, but with banks provided with deposit insurance and guarantees of their liabilities while nonbank affiliates are not so blessed, the benefits of basing activities in banks rather than nonbank affiliates will, in many instances, exceed the costs. Insulation will probably diminish rather than increase because the activities of many nonbank subsidiaries will end up in banks.

## New Powers for Banking Organizations

The current approach to bank and holding company regulation will not be viable in the long run as banking organizations are granted new powers. Unless explicitly prohibited, each new activity that involves position taking of one kind or another is likely to end up in banks (or bank subsidiaries), not in nonbank subsidiaries. That in turn will mean that the federal safety net will be cast under an ever-larger number of activities. Unless something is done to arrest that trend, the government could end up trying to protect and guarantee virtually every kind of financial activity.

The potential problem has been recognized to some extent and is one justification for proposals to require that new activities be conducted by nonbank affiliates rather than by banks themselves. In principle that would deprive those activities of the protection of the federal safety net. Unfortunately, that approach is not viable if nonbank affiliates are subject to banklike regulation. Banking organizations will find it very difficult to compete in the provision of underwriting services for corporate securities and other activities if they are subject to arbitrary capital requirements, forced to serve as sources of strength for affiliated banks, and faced with other restrictions that are not inflicted on competitors that are not affiliated with a bank. To go down that path is to grant banking organizations new powers that probably will not be used.

It appears much more desirable to eliminate the special restrictions and regulations that are currently imposed on nonbank entities within holding companies. Those entities should be subject to no more regulation than are firms that provide the same services outside banking organizations. There should be no prudential regulation or supervision of their activities by the Federal Reserve or any other banking authority, and there should be no government-imposed capital requirements. Such treatment of nonbank entities affiliated with banks is feasible and desirable precisely because banks within holding companies can be insulated. With insulation, the bank is protected and there is no economic justification for regulating the nonbank parts of holding companies. Organizations that own banks can enter new activities on a competitive basis without endangering the bank, *provided* the bank is effectively insulated.

### What Is Banking?

Bank insulation is a powerful tool only if nonbanking activities are unprotected and kept out of the clutches of the bank regulators. But what is banking and what is nonbanking? In the modern world the answer to that question is far from obvious. One approach to the issue is to arbitrarily define any activity that banks currently engage in as banking and conversely to define all other activities as nonbanking. There is a superficial appeal to the banks-are-what-banks-currently-do definition, and that definition seems to underlie proposals to eliminate the prohibitions of the Glass-

Steagall Act and require banking organizations to exercise their new securities powers through nonbank subsidiaries.

That approach would lead to some anomalous behavior, however. Banks could continue to underwrite general obligation bonds of states and municipalities, but revenue bonds issued by those same entities would have to be underwritten by a nonbank subsidiary, because banks cannot now underwrite revenue bonds. Similarly, banks could continue to deal in government securities, foreign exchange, and interest rate swaps, and they could engage in full securities activities abroad, but their domestic corporate securities activities would have to be conducted through a nonbank subsidiary. The same sort of strange mixture would occur if banking organizations were granted full insurance powers. For example, a bank could underwrite credit life insurance, but only a nonbank subsidiary could provide general life insurance.

Perhaps even more important, requiring that all new activities be conducted through nonbank affiliates would keep banks from offering new products. Banks would become increasingly obsolete and noncompetitive. Furthermore, it would probably prove inefficient for holding companies to continue to engage in currently allowed securities and insurance activities within their banks while conducting new activities through nonbanks. In many instances, holding companies would simply move currently allowed activities out of banks into nonbanks. Such consolidation could be profitable for the holding company, but it would cut some banks off from important sources of earnings. That does not trouble me particularly, but it is likely to displease the regulators who might then press to allow banks to engage in the new activities. If the regulators were successful, the federal safety net would effectively be extended to all securities activities and insurance.

### The Role of the Federal Safety Net

The federal safety net is the linchpin of the resolution of the bank insulation issue. Since 1933 when the safety net was put in place, banks have expanded the variety of liabilities they issue till today they offer money market instruments worldwide. In addition, banks have acquired a vast array of assets, and they have developed a seemingly endless variety of off-balance-sheet activities. As banks have expanded and evolved, the government has transformed the safety net program from one that insured small depositors and protected the banking system from liquidity crises to one through which the government protects creditors of all kinds at virtually all banks. Only when the smallest banks fail are insured depositors paid off and uninsured depositors and creditors exposed to loss. All other bank failures are handled by takeovers that protect all creditors. Typically, that involves the Federal Reserve's providing emergency credit, which is secured by the bank's assets and ultimately by the FDIC, to a failing bank until the FDIC can arrange a subsidized purchase of the bank's assets and assumption of all its liabilities by another banking organization.

The perversion of the safety net into a program that bails out insolvent banks and protects uninsured creditors must be dealt with soon. If it is not, the safety net will be spread under an increasing number of activities, and banking organizations will shift more risk to the government and the taxpayers.

### Redefining What a Bank Is

If agreement can be reached on precisely what functions are so important that they should be protected and regulated, the bank insulation issue can be used to reverse the tendency to protect more and more activities. Institutions that provide those functions should be classified as banks. They should be allowed to engage in those functions and no others, because to allow them to do more would mean that the safety net would end up protecting other activities as well.

The newly defined banks should be permitted to affiliate with providers of other financial services, but the banks should be effectively insulated from their affiliates' misfortunes. The nonbank parts of financial services companies should receive no protection from the government, nor should they be subject to the regulation currently imposed on bank holding companies. Financial services holding companies and their affiliates would be subject, of course, to the antitrust, securities, and other statutes that are now in place.

But what banking functions are so crucial that they should receive federal protection and regulation? An extended discussion is beyond the scope of this paper, but a few comments are in order.[10] Banks are crucial to the provision of monetary services, including the provision of transaction accounts (accounts that are payable on demand at par as cash withdrawals or payments to third parties) and the payment system itself. Those are the activities that the federal safety net was intended to protect so that collapses of the money supply, and the credit system it supports, could not occur again as they did in the 1930s.

Monetary functions are difficult to protect today because there are so many uses to which banks can put their funds, and many of those uses are quite risky. Furthermore, when funds raised through transaction accounts are commingled with those obtained by issuing time accounts, negotiable CDs, Eurodebt, and other liabilities, it proves difficult in practice to protect transaction accounts without protecting all of the other liabilities as well.

It appears that the cleanest approach is to restrict banks to the provision of transaction accounts, which are fully insured, and to the acquisition of assets that are highly liquid and low risk. But I part company with Litan (1987) and others who would limit those assets to short-term government securities or the equivalent. That would be overly restrictive because it would reduce and distort the provision of credit to private borrowers. Risk is sufficiently low if banks are limited to purchases of highly rated money market instruments, including commercial and financial paper, and if they are required to achieve minimum standards of diversification. Under those conditions, bank risk can be easily insured, monitored, and controlled. To assure the public that its money is safe, deposit insurance for banks should be provided by the federal government and financed by appropriate fees on banks. The newly defined banks would not be allowed to provide daylight overdrafts and would operate the payment system with "good funds."

Thus, banking should be narrowly defined, and all other activities that are currently conducted by banks should revert to uninsured, unprotected, and unregulated nonbanking organizations.[11] Banks could be affiliated with institutions that provide other financial services, and the affiliation would be regulated only to the extent necessary to insulate banks from the misfortunes of their affiliates.

Private market discipline would replace government regulation in the management of nonbank affiliates. The market would impose capital requirements and risk premiums. The good name of the bank would in no way be threatened by misfortunes of nonbank affiliates. If a financial conglomerate found it in its interest to support a troubled component, it would be free to do so, provided that its affiliated banks were insulated.

The approach proposed here would make it easy to handle the question of securities powers of banks. Financial services companies would be free to offer whatever securities services they chose. Their activities would be limited only by economic conditions and securities statutes. Banks as redefined could not engage in securities activities of any kind, but they could be affiliated with businesses that did. Information, personnel, and physical capital could be shared, but the bank would be insulated from any losses suffered by its securities affiliates.

It would be naive to believe that such a fundamental restructuring of banking and its regulation can be achieved quickly or easily, but a beginning, at least, can be made. All that is needed is to require that any new powers for banking organizations be exercised by nonbank affiliates *and* that neither the Federal Reserve nor any other bank regulator have any jurisdiction over those affiliates. Furthermore, to underscore its commitment to bank insulation, Congress should eliminate loopholes and ambiguities in current restrictions on transactions between banks and nonbank affiliates and substantially increase the penalties for breaking the law.

## The Role of the Federal Reserve

Insulating banks from securities affiliates is more difficult than it might appear because the Federal Reserve is sure to oppose it. Many members of Congress will also be opposed either because they have been convinced by the Fed that it is impossible to insulate banks or because they find the Federal Reserve's position a convenient excuse for continuing to protect their securities and insurance industry constituents.

Bank insulation and meaningful new powers for banking organizations cannot be achieved unless the Federal Reserve is either won over or neutralized. Once it is recognized that banks can be insulated from the misfortunes of their nonbank affiliates, there is no good reason for the Fed to regulate those affiliates. It is unlikely that the Fed will change its collective mind or its lobbying efforts, however, because to do so would involve a considerable erosion of its power and prestige. The Federal Reserve is unlikely to accept such a loss of influence willingly.[12]

The Federal Reserve's position on the matter was clearly spelled out by Keeley and Bennett (1988, p. 3) in a recent publication of the Federal Reserve Bank of San Francisco:

> The powers of banking organizations can and should be expanded, but stronger regulation, including capital regulation, of banks and their holding companies is needed to protect the insurance system. Corporate separateness alone provides some protection, but needs to be supplemented with regulation of the consolidated organization.

That statement indicates that even if the Fed were kept from directly regulating securities affiliates, it would attempt to regulate them indirectly through capital requirements and other measures directed at the "consolidated organization." That position is unfortunate because bank insulation cannot become a practical reality until the Federal Reserve is taken out of the business of regulating nonbank affiliates.

## Notes

1. For extended discussions of this point see Cox (1986), Cooper and Fraser (1986), Litan (1987), Pierce (1991), and Walter (1985).

2. The Federal Deposit Insurance Act contains restrictions parallel to those of the Federal Reserve Act to cover insured nonmember banks.

3. In the event that bank holding companies were granted additional securities powers, it would be even more important that daylight overdrafts be included in this definition because securities firms are heavy users of electronic payment systems.

4. Banks use deposits and other liabilities to support asset holdings that are a large multiple of their equity (net worth); that is, leverage. Holding companies, in turn, as owners of banks and their net worth, issue additional debt and obtain even greater leverage; that is, double leverage.

5. In addition, the safety net should be limited even for banks, and even large banks should be subject to failure, but that is a separate issue.

6. Unless the Federal Reserve forces the transfer of resources, an event that should not be allowed.

7. Those issues are discussed more fully in Pierce (1988).

8. Those topics are discussed in detail in Chase, Laub and Company (1987).

9. Although the discussion here concerns banking organizations, it should be noted that it is common outside banking to establish limited liability for separate companies within a "corporate family." For example, General Motors Acceptance Corporation, a captive finance company, is not responsible for the liabilities of the parent, General Motors Corporation, or for any other part of the complex General Motors corporate structure. Similarly, the operating subsidiaries of Texaco, Inc., were not affected when their parent declared bankruptcy during its legal war with Pennzoil.

10. See Pierce (1991).

11. By "unregulated" I mean no bank or bank holding company regulation. Existing statutes that cover the conduct of financial and nonfinancial firms would apply.

12. Those issues are discussed more fully in Pierce (1990).

## References

Chase, Laub & Company. 1987. "Insulating Banks from Risks Run by Nonbank Affiliates." Paper prepared for the American Bankers Association, Washington, D.C., October.

Cooper, Kerry, and Fraser, Donald. 1986. *Banking Deregulation and the New Competition in Financial Services*. Cambridge, Mass.: Ballinger.

Cox, Edwin. 1986. "The Changing Role of Banks in the Financial Services Industry." In *The Bank Director's Handbook*. 2d ed. Dover, Mass.: Auburn House.

Keeley, Michael C., and Bennett, Barbara A. 1988. "Corporate Separateness." Federal Reserve Bank of San Francisco *Weekly Letter*, June 2.

Litan, Robert. 1987. *What Should Banks Do?* Washington, D.C.: Brookings Institution.

Pierce, James L. 1988. "Integrating Banking with Other Financial Services." In *Regulating the New Financial Services Industry*, edited by Cynthia Glassman et al., pp. 25–44. Washington, D.C.: Center for National Policy Press.

Pierce, James L. 1990. "The Federal Reserve as a Political Power." In *The Political Economy of American Monetary Policy*, edited by Thomas Mayer, pp. 193–215. New York: Cambridge University Press.

Pierce, James L. 1991. *The Future of Banking*. New Haven, Conn.: Yale University Press.

Walter, Ingo, ed. 1985. *Deregulating Wall Street*. New York: John Wiley and Sons.

Wriston, Walter. 1981. Statement before the Senate Committee on Banking, Housing and Urban Affairs, 97th Cong. 1st Sess. In *Financial Institutions Restructuring and Services Act of 1981*, pp. 427–688. Washington, D.C.: Government Printing Office.

# 6 BANKS ARE NOT SPECIAL: THE FEDERAL SAFETY NET AND BANKING POWERS

Walker F. Todd

The purpose of this paper is to stimulate reconsideration of fundamental principles in the debate on the restructuring of the financial services industry. Four underlying propositions are defended:

1.  Public moneys should not be used to subsidize the risk-taking activities of depository institutions.
2.  The lender of last resort should confine its activities to lending to support the short-term liquidity needs of depository institutions and should not engage in equity investment or capital replacement for banks or thrift institutions.

The author is a grantee of the Gulliver Foundation, San Francisco, California. At the time the paper was written he was assistant general counsel and research officer of the Federal Reserve Bank of Cleveland. The views presented are entirely his own and do not represent the official views of the Gulliver Foundation, the Federal Reserve Bank of Cleveland, or the Board of Governors of the Federal Reserve System. This paper was initially presented at the conference, and has since been referenced in several places, under the title, "No Conspiracy, but a Convenient Forgetting: Dr. Pangloss Visits the World of Deposit Insurance."

79

3.  The deposit insurance laws should be strictly construed to reduce
    moral hazard and to avoid favoring one class of institutions or claimants
    over other classes.
4.  The central bank should neither monetize the Treasury's deficits nor
    make payments that either would not be made or would be made by
    the Treasury if the central bank did not make them.

Such restrictions on the central bank's payments are necessary both to
avoid credit allocation (central planning) and to enable Congress to
maintain proper control over (political accountability for) the spending of
public moneys.

## Background

The underlying premise herein is that banks' risk-taking activities should
not be subsidized by any agency of the federal government. That is the
reason for examining the prospects for effectively insulating banks' risk
taking from the federal safety net. However, the other three propositions
are inextricably linked to the first as well as to each other.

In the present political environment, the principle of avoiding public
subsidies of private risk taking has faded from view. Virtually no one in a
policymaking or policy-influencing position today appears to understand
the applicability of that principle to policy questions regarding banks or
savings-and-loan associations. The present state of affairs is all the more
distressing because many political economists who have read Adam Smith
and who claim to be libertarians, conservatives, or Smithian laissez-faire
economists still believe that state (or central bank) subsidies of certain
forms of private-sector risk taking by depository institutions are desirable,
or at least inevitable. Given today's environment, taxpayers told that
"banks are special" should reach for their wallets to make sure they are
still there.

A lot of influential people are expending a lot of financial and political
capital to preserve the current deposit insurance environment. If we
examine their stance closely, we quickly discover that, although the
present deposit insurance systems exhibit serious fundamental flaws,
maintaining credibility with the general public requires that one appear to
wholeheartedly accept federal deposit insurance as basically sound and
suppress any inconvenient contradictory facts or logical deductions. Although there is not (yet) any active conspiracy to suppress skeptics, it does
seem to observers from outside Washington that many pertinent facts and
deductions have been conveniently forgotten by policymakers.

## Definition of Terms

It may be instructive to define some of the terms commonly used in discussions of the proper role of depository institutions and the federal safety net.

In central banking parlance, "liquidity support" is understood to mean the extension of short-term, fully secured credit at current market value (or at face or par value for certain types of government securities). "Solvency" requires positive marked-to-market-value net worth. It is sometimes argued that solvency is a meaningless term and that all shortages of funds are liquidity problems only.[1] However, thrift industry practice has historically been to deem insolvent any institution that cannot pay its creditors at par within 60 days. With respect to banks, the "self-liquidating commercial paper" criterion applied to collateral for loans from the Federal Reserve Banks' discount window implies that a commercial bank unable to meet its obligations to deposit customers within 90 days should be considered insolvent.

The capital (or net worth) of depository institutions should always be positive. Although industrial companies with large amounts of depreciated fixed assets sometimes may operate successfully with deeply negative net worth, industrial enterprises usually do not operate under exclusive governmental licenses akin to bank charters. Nor do industrial companies enjoy the equivalent of federal deposit insurance whereby they can create liabilities guaranteed by the federal government. Thus, although banks are not special enough to deserve a governmental subsidy of their risk taking, they are different from industrial enterprises when it comes to the consequences of negative net worth.

A "bailout" is a publicly funded rescue from financial difficulties without full and adequate security for the public's advance of funds. Bailouts usually involve a government agency's replacing private-sector debt with its own claim. The government agency also generally agrees to lengthen the maturities of the unstable institution's obligations.[2] In a bailout the government allows the troubled bank considerably more time to repay its debts than would a private creditor. When the maturity of the government-supplied loan extends into the distant future, no useful economic or common-sense distinctions remain between debt (or liquidity assistance) and an infusion of government-supplied equity (or solvency support). For all practical purposes the government's loan has become a capital investment. In other words, a bailout may be said to occur when public funds are used to enable a depository institution to carry assets currently incapable of liquidation at par for periods in excess of some reasonably brief time (usually less than a year).[3] As a matter of common sense and custom, 10 or

20 years of debt relief cannot be considered temporary liquidity assistance.

The "lender of last resort" is any institution (typically the central bank) with ultimate responsibility for providing gold, silver, legal tender paper currency, or central bank reserves in exchange for nonmonetary assets to the extent of its capacity to do so. In the United States, the LLR typically provides liquidity, not solvency or capital support, to depository institutions. At various times in U.S. history, several entities have acted as an LLR: the Treasury, the First and Second Banks of the United States, the New York Clearing House Association, J. P. Morgan, August Belmont, the Federal Reserve Banks, and the Reconstruction Finance Corporation.

The RFC, which was authorized in March 1933 to provide solvency or capital assistance to depository institutions, represents an exception to the general rule of favoring liquidity support only.[4] Since 1982 the Federal Deposit Insurance Corporation and the Federal Home Loan Bank System, including the Federal Savings and Loan Insurance Corporation, have had RFC-like powers to provide either liquidity or solvency (capital) support to member institutions.

### A Bad Idea

The use of public moneys to subsidize the risk-taking activities of depository institutions is a bad idea. Todd (1988) makes and elaborates on the following principal points:

1.  The traditional and peculiarly American theory of the LLR prohibits using public moneys to subsidize private-sector risk taking, especially risk taking by banks. Though urgent fiscal necessity, at least as perceived at the time, led to creation of the First and Second Banks of the United States in the pre–Civil War era, the affairs of those early national banks were conducted with sufficient prudence that their operations caused no loss to the Treasury.[5]
2.  The moral prohibition against public bailouts of or subsidies for private enterprises, though imperfectly observed, persisted into the 20th century. At the federal level, the principal breaches of fiscal discipline occurred during financial panics (e.g., 1857, 1873, and 1893) when the Treasury deposited funds in the banking system despite explicit legal prohibitions after 1846 against such deposits. The principle was undermined further when national banks were created in 1863 both to absorb Treasury securities during the Civil War and to issue bank notes (i.e., incur liabilities) against pledges of Treasury securities.[6]

The Great Depression (1929–41) brought the large-scale bailout issue to a head, and in 1932 the Hoover administration chartered the RFC to supply solvency or capital support to businesses in general and to banks in particular. The Roosevelt administration expanded the activities of the RFC in 1933.[7] After 1933 the security pledged for RFC assistance was generally adequate. In addition, the Federal Reserve Banks were entirely removed from the RFC's operations. The central bank could neither fund the RFC directly by making loans to it, nor could the Fed provide indirect assistance by accepting RFC obligations as collateral for advances to member banks.

When the FDIC was established in 1933, Congress required the Federal Reserve to contribute approximately one-half of the FDIC's initial capitalization. However, the ongoing operations of the FDIC were separate from those of the Fed, and there is no evidence that the central bank was intended to make new advances to the FDIC after the initial capital contribution. Nor does the Federal Reserve have explicit statutory authority to make capital contributions to the Federal Home Loan Bank System or the FSLIC. Both the FDIC and the FSLIC do have explicit statutory authority to borrow directly from the Treasury, apparently for liquidity purposes.[8] Thus, if the deposit insurance funds require a new infusion of liquidity or capital, both statute and precedent suggest that the Treasury, pursuant to politically accountable, explicit congressional authorization, should provide the assistance, not the central bank.

Economic reasoning and common sense also suggest that should be the case. If the Treasury provides assistance to the deposit insurance funds, then political accountability for the use of those moneys is established (the Treasury can expend funds or borrow money only pursuant to congressionally approved appropriations or authorizations), and the public debate on the expenditure occurs *before* the funds are disbursed. On the other hand, if the central bank provides the funds, there is no public debate before disbursement, there is no direct congressional control of expenditures, and the particulars of an expenditure may not be disclosed clearly to the public. Treasury assistance to the deposit insurance funds is a bad idea, but it is better than central bank assistance.

### Short-Term Liquidity Assistance

The LLR should provide only short-term liquidity assistance to depository institutions and should not engage in equity investment or capital support.

The LLR, strictly speaking, is a *lender*, not an *investor*. The Fed has a responsibility to confine assistance to the short-term provision of liquidity on a fully secured, market value basis. Arguments by the Fed that its exposure to risk of loss will be brief, that it is simply engaged in "bridge financing," or that the "loan" will quickly be placed either with the Treasury or with private investors should be viewed as suspect if the central bank's loan is less than fully secured or if the collateral value reported on the books of the LLR exceeds market value. A central bank advance for which the timing and source of ultimate repayment cannot be forecast with reasonable certainty at the time the advance is made acquires the color of a bailout loan, regardless of how it is characterized. Moreover, if a "lend first and ask questions later" policy is adopted as a general rule, the official terminology will have to be revised to LFR—lender of first resort—to reflect the underlying realities of the situation.

Logically, LFR assistance, bridge loans, open-ended "temporary liquidity assistance," equity investment, and capital support or replacement by public entities all constitute credit allocation. Credit allocation and guided investment are typical of centrally planned economies, the economies of some developing countries, and highly developed economies with mercantilistic tendencies. Similarly, government-sponsored efforts to use central bank subsidies to prevent the failures that naturally result from competition are characteristic of developing or socialist countries. There seems to be no logically or theoretically useful role for such central planning or credit allocation in a nominally open, market-oriented economy like that of the United States.

It is therefore astonishing to hear some of the free market's purportedly strongest defenders making lame excuses for government bailouts today. Corporate welfare subsidies are not only as unproductive as individual welfare subsidies, they also cost more and often are harder to abolish than are programs for individuals. Central planning and its bailout lending component are habit forming; once the first step has been taken, even temporarily and in the most urgent of circumstances, it is hard to turn back.[9] The precedent created by one breach of LLR discipline inevitably is raised in public debates when policymakers consider other requests for bailouts. These days the usual litany is Lockheed–New York City–Chrysler–Continental Illinois, as though one inevitably led to or justified the next. It appears that there is no such thing as a non-precedent-setting bailout.

The LLR's dilemma, if that is what it is, in deciding to breach precedent and deny a new bailout request is like the one Secretary of State Thomas Jefferson (1975, pp. 261–62) posed to President George Washington in 1791 regarding the constitutionality of the national bank charter:

To take a single step beyond the boundaries thus specially drawn [by the Constitution] around the powers of Congress, is to take possession of a boundless field of power, no longer susceptible of any definition.

That is, a precedent once established cannot easily be broken. If Congress chartered a national bank in 1791 that was unnecessary for the accomplishment of a specifically enumerated power of Congress, then Congress later could build upon that precedent by chartering more such banks or doing a host of other things neither strictly necessary nor specifically enumerated. Similarly, an LLR that once makes equity investments in a private firm crosses a line on the other side of which it becomes possible with increasing frequency to spend ever larger amounts of public money and allocate credit without adequate political accountability for those actions.

## Strict Construction

The deposit insurance law should be construed strictly to reduce moral hazard and favoritism. The FDIC historically has had a great deal of difficulty in limiting its outlays in bank failures to only the principal amounts of insured deposits. The FDIC initially protected deposits to $2,500.[10] Under the original plan, the FDIC was expected to operate only as a receiver, liquidating agent, or conservator of national and state member banks. It was to estimate the probable recovery from the estate of a failed bank and to use that information to determine the size of depositors' accounts in the new bank organized by the FDIC to pay off insured claims. The FDIC's liquidation expenses were to be deducted from the amounts ultimately distributed to depositors, and the FDIC was authorized to retain for itself any funds recovered in excess of the original estimates.[11] Furthermore, in its early days, any time the FDIC's reserve fund fell below 0.25 percent of the deposit liabilities of all insured institutions, the insurer had the right to assess an additional premium to cover the deficiency. In other words, the FDIC was intended to operate more or less along the lines of a mutual insurance fund. To avoid burdening its healthy members, no rational mutual insurance fund would pay more than its contractual obligations for insured deposits, after taking account of estimated recoveries.

The 1934 amendments to the FDIC's enabling legislation increased federal deposit insurance from $2,500 to $5,000 per insured depositor.[12] The act was further amended at least once each year from 1935 through 1939. The amendments began to replace many of the self-correcting, moral hazard–reducing features of the original insurance plan with blanket coverage, though the limit remained $5,000 per depositor for some time.

The comparatively low bank failure rate after the FDIC was established may have contributed to that transition. In retrospect, few if any banks should have been closed for reasons other than gross insolvency between 1933 and 1947, because the RFC made advances to and purchased non-voting stock from banks with insufficient capital.[13] Although nearly 5,000 commercial banks failed to reopen after the March 1933 emergency bank holiday, in the first seven years of its operations, 1934 through 1940, the FDIC experienced only 355 bank failures.[14] The maximum loss to the FDIC in any one year during the period was 29.5 percent of its disbursements in 1935. By 1940 the insurer had reduced that loss to 4.3 percent (Federal Deposit Insurance Corporation 1987, p. 62, Table 125).

Since those early days, maximum FDIC insurance coverage has increased from $5,000 to its current limit of $100,000 per account (Table 6–1). Despite legislated ceilings on coverage, the FDIC has usually succeeded in arranging complete or nearly complete payoffs to all depositors, both insured and uninsured, by relying on assisted mergers and purchase-and-assumption agreements to resolve most bank failures. In 1950, when the FDIC lost an amount equal to 31.4 percent of the insured deposits in only four bank failures, Congress sent the FDIC a clear message: stop trying to pay off everyone with assisted mergers and purchase-and-assumption agreements. In return for expected adherence to those instructions, Congress agreed to increase the deposit insurance maximum from $5,000 to $10,000 per account. As Caliguire and Thomson (1987) put it, in 1950 Congress named

> the cost test . . . explicitly as the primary criterion for determining FDIC action in individual bank failures. Congress felt that such a restatement of purpose was a necessary reminder to the FDIC that its mission was not to eliminate bank failures, but to dispose of failed banks in the least costly and most efficient manner.

The FDIC's repeated backsliding on its commitment to retain market discipline in the resolution of bank failures and recurring surges in the FDIC's losses from failure resolutions forced Congress periodically to repeat its message of 1950. The deal was always the same: Congress reminded the FDIC that it was supposed to consider the cost of a complete rescue of depositors before committing itself to such a rescue, and in return, Congress raised the deposit insurance limit. FDIC losses (as a percentage of its disbursements) and the dates and amounts of increased deposit insurance coverage are given in Table 6–1.

Table 6-1. FDIC Losses vs. Increased Insurance Coverage

| Year of Loss | Loss on Disbursements (%) | Year of Increase | Increased Limit ($) |
|---|---|---|---|
| 1948 | 20.3 | 1934 | (was 5,000) |
| 1949 | 13.7 | – | – |
| 1950 | 31.4 | 1950 | 10,000 |
| 1952 | 51.9 | – | – |
| 1954 | 25.1 | – | – |
| 1961 | 24.2 | – | – |
| 1964 | 11.2 | – | – |
| 1965 | 33.7 | – | – |
| 1966 | 2.4 | 1966 | 15,000 |
| 1967 | 12.5 | – | – |
| 1969 | 0.2 | 1969 | 20,000 |
| 1972 | 11.1 | – | – |
| 1973 | 15.5 | – | – |
| 1974 | 0.0 | 1974 | 40,000 |
| 1979 | 11.7 | – | – |
| 1980 | 20.6 | 1980 | 100,000 |
| 1981 | 58.7 | – | – |
| 1982 | 57.4 | – | –[a] |
| 1983 | 48.5 | – | – |
| 1984 | 31.5 | – | – |
| 1985 | 36.1 | – | – |
| 1986 | 47.6 | – | –[b] |
| 1987 | 46.3 | – | – |

*Sources:* FDIC, *Annual Report 1986*, p. 62 (Table 125) for 1948–86, and FDIC *Annual Report 1987*, p. 61 (Table 125) for 1987.

*Note:* Losses were more than offset by the FDIC's income from investments and assessments for every year after 1934. Only losses in excess of 10 percent of the FDIC's disbursements are presented here for years in which there was no increase in deposit insurance coverage.

[a] Net worth assistance was authorized by Congress in 1982.

[b] The FSLIC's net worth assistance authority expired in October 1986 but was renewed and extended until October 13, 1991.

Although the FDIC's losses on resolutions of bank failures have been running at record levels throughout the 1980s, both in nominal dollars and as a percentage of disbursements, Congress has not reacted as it did in the past. Specifically, Congress has not reminded the FDIC of its obligation to minimize the cost to the insurance fund when choosing among modified payouts, straight payments of insured amounts only, open-bank assistance, assisted mergers, or purchase-and-assumption agreements. Instead, in 1982 Congress authorized the FDIC to provide net worth assistance. In 1987 that authority was renewed at the same time Congress expanded the insurer's ability to conduct an open-bank assistance program.

It appears that Congress and the federal bank supervisory and regulatory authorities have forgotten, conveniently perhaps, both the original purpose of federal deposit insurance and the adjustments necessary to correct the system if it is to avoid mathematical, actuarial, and fiscal disaster.[15] The recently acquired and expanded *solvency* or capital support authority of the FDIC and the FSLIC resembles the solvency support powers of the RFC during its heyday (1933–47). It is not at all clear, however, that the administration, congressional leaders, or their staffs were consciously trying to reactivate the RFC by way of the 1982 and 1987 amendments of the deposit insurance statutes.[16] Those who would recreate the RFC or give RFC-like powers to other governmental agencies and instrumentalities should keep in mind the following points:

1. The original RFC was completely separate from the central bank and did not rely on the central bank for its funds.
2. Solvency or capital support efforts of the federal government, including loans to support liquidation of closed banks, were channeled through the RFC, not through the central bank.
3. When the FDIC required a new infusion of cash after the initial round of bank failure resolutions in 1934, Congress required the RFC (not the central bank) to purchase up to $250 million of FDIC obligations at par.

Thus, if the deposit insurance agencies require new loans to carry out their deposit insurance functions, the relevant precedent suggests that (a) the central bank should not lend to support those functions,[17] (b) Congress should appropriate any moneys required, and (c) an entity with the powers of the RFC can lend to the deposit insurance funds, but the central bank cannot do so under existing statutes.

The parade of federal bailouts in the 1970s and 1980s and the central bank's involvement in funding several of those bailouts may be interpreted by some observers as indications that there is nothing wrong with using such measures to solve the problems of the deposit insurance funds. Some would argue that, since the precedent already exists, it should be taken advantage of whenever political convenience, disguised as economic necessity, requires it. That position, however, is based on an imperfect understanding of economic reasoning, custom, law, and common sense.

For example, there were no actual federal outlays in the rescues of the 1970s. Franklin National Bank (1974) ultimately was liquidated with no direct loss to the FDIC.[18] Only in the 1980s has the rescue of large financial institutions caused substantial (hundreds of millions of dollars) losses to the FDIC and the FSLIC.[19] In the recent series of large rescues, only in the cases of Franklin, Continental Illinois, First City, First Republic, and Financial Corporation of America were uninsured depositors and other uninsured claimants paid off either at par or at a value in excess of the market value of their claims on the closing or rescue dates.

The last point may become increasingly significant in future bank and savings-and-loan rescue efforts. According to the FDIC's 1988 *Annual Report*, 75.1 percent of all insured banks' deposits fall under the $100,000 deposit insurance ceiling.[20] Current numbers on the coverage of thrift institution deposits by the FSLIC are difficult to find, but the FSLIC probably covers at least an equal percentage of thrift institution deposits, if not more.[21]

The trend toward expanding deposit insurance coverage is clear.[22] The resulting increase in moral hazard could, however, be tolerated if the deposit insurance laws were construed strictly and if political and economic pressures to further expand deposit insurance coverage could be resisted. That does not seem to be the case. In recent bank failures, it has been routine practice to pay off uninsured depositors at par. That de facto policy is especially disturbing because insured deposits in large banks typically constitute only a small percentage of all deposits. The six largest New York Clearing House banks, for example, rely principally on wholesale and foreign branch or subsidiary funding sources. At year-end 1986 their insured deposits, as a percentage of total domestic deposits, ranged from 12.32 to 58.90 percent. Their insured deposits, as a percentage of total deposits (including uninsured foreign branch or subsidiary deposits), ranged from 3.48 to 32.73 percent.[23] But the "too big to fail" doctrine was conceived in 1982–84 to deal with cases just like those.[24]

Although it might make some economic or logical sense to have the FDIC rescue banks that have all or almost all of their deposits insured, it is difficult to understand the reasons for rescuing banks that have less than one-third of their deposits insured. Such rescues raise the ugly specters of central planning and governmental favoritism as taxpayers are called on to protect persons whose deposits are, for the most part, legally uninsured.

It will be difficult enough for taxpayers to cover the expected losses of the FSLIC on fully insured deposits; it will become even more expensive if, as the result of either an explicit or an implicit expansion of the federal safety net, taxpayers are asked to guarantee deposits that are now uninsured.

Next April 15 taxpayers should stop to remember that a $100 billion FSLIC rescue works out to $1,000 per tax return—far more than most taxpayers currently have in insured deposits. Such expenditures of tax moneys cannot be justifed by sound economic reasoning, yet the political wisdom in Washington has clearly been to do nothing about deposit insurance and the federal safety net. But is doing nothing, or appointing politically sensitive commissions to study the problem while it becomes worse, an acceptable solution?

The deposit insurance laws must be strictly construed if we are to reduce to a bearable minimum the cost to taxpayers of maintaining the federal safety net yet preserve the benefits of the efficiency gains produced by deregulation and inflict the harsh discipline of the marketplace on the truly deserving.[25]

No class of claimants (e.g., uninsured depositors) should receive more favorable treatment (e.g., higher rates on deposits with full protection of principal and interest) than do other classes of claimants (e.g., insured depositors) at public expense. A system established to protect domestic retail depositors should not be abused to provide below-market-rate funding options to wholesale (brokered, insured certificates of deposit) and foreign branch or subsidiary deposit takers. Each insured depositor should be allowed only one trip to the well; a securities firm that moves brokered certificates of deposit from one failing institution to another should not be paid in full each time.

### What Central Banks Should Not Do

Central banks should not monetize the Treasury's deficits, should not make payments that the private sector would not make voluntarily in the absence of explicit statutory authorization, and should not make payments on unsecured debts to third parties for the Treasury's account.

The general outlines of the arguments in support of that proposition were suggested earlier.[26] The proposition that the central bank's monetization of the Treasury's deficits is a major step down the road to increased inflation is supported by legal and common-sense arguments, three of which are especially important in U.S. history and tradition:

1.  Such monetization was never intended, except during a declared war, before 1933.
2.  The pre-1933 wartime monetizations of Treasury deficits always con-

templated an eventual return to a gold or bimetallic standard, and the normal customs and excise taxes were accompanied by increased levels of federal income taxation (during and after the Civil War).

3. Since 1933, and especially since 1947, the monetization of deficits has been only a temporary expedient, the authorization for which generally expired within one to three years.

Finance ministers throughout history have attempted to use central banks to monetize treasury deficits. Acutely aware of that, the Framers of the Constitution provided that all legislation dealing with taxes must originate in the House of Representatives, the chamber closest to the taxpaying public. The Founders also gave Congress sole authority to approve the borrowing of money on the credit of the United States and to coin money and regulate its value. Those steps were taken to frustrate any future treasury secretary's attempt to circumvent the checks and balances on governmental spending by attempting to borrow money on his sole authority, by issuing coin or currency, or by depreciating the value of money without prior congressional approval. The creation of a central bank does not alter the calculus very much (even though Alexander Hamilton thought that the bank's "convenient loans" to the Treasury were a sufficient rationale for chartering the First Bank of the United States).[27]

Federal Reserve assistance to the deposit insurance funds is an equally important issue. Bank insurance agencies might be tempted to seek indirect aid by asking one or more of the Federal Reserve Banks to accept delayed repayment of advances to depository institutions acquired by the deposit insurer. In traditional central banking theory, the central bank could provide only limited assistance to the deposit insurer because the gold standard constrained even the central bank. Advances to a deposit insurer in excess of the central bank's specie or bullion reserves might cause the illiquidity (suspension of redemption in specie) of the central bank's circulating notes (paper currency). Indeed, if the central bank were so imprudent as to advance funds to the deposit insurer without adequate security, the central bank itself could become insolvent and face liquidation, an eventuality for which the Federal Reserve Act explicitly provides.

In a gold standard world, responding to a central bank's insolvency could also entail significant social costs. The Treasury would need either to recapitalize the central bank through a public debt issue or a tax increase or to liquidate the central bank, which might entail paying off its obligations at less than par.

In the absence of the gold standard, it is unlikely that the Federal Reserve would be effectively bankrupted by aiding the deposit insurers, but fundamental reasons exist for prohibiting the central bank from postponing recognition of a deposit insurer's insolvency:

1. It is simple textbook political economy that the central bank should not subordinate its credit decisions to the Treasury's need to finance its deficits. To do so weakens fiscal discipline and threatens inflation. The same principle applies to central bank funding of the Treasury's indirect deficits, that is, the obligations of government agencies or instrumentalities that the Treasury would have to finance elsewhere if the central bank did not fund them. In addition, the central bank should refrain from making payments that the private sector would not make voluntarily. Not only do such payments amount to a form of credit allocation, they lack the element of anonymity that is a key feature of the most effective and sustainable central bank monetary operations. Central bank financing of government agency debts, including obligations of a deposit insurer, is not assistance that must be provided of *necessity*. To be sure, many government officials would find it very *convenient* to avoid their responsibility to either recapitalize or liquidate large financial institutions or government-sponsored credit agencies. However, precisely because the central bank's assistance would spare political figures hard choices in those cases, political accountability to the general public would be lost.

2. In addition to being bad fiscal policy, it would be bad law for the Federal Reserve to fund the government or its agencies other than by provision of central bank credit for full-faith-and-credit government obligations in the open market. The Federal Reserve Act provides explicitly that the Federal Reserve Banks may purchase the Treasury's obligations only in the open market, *not* directly from the Treasury.

3. Lending to the Treasury indirectly, by lending to a deposit insurer or a government agency under one of the emergency lending provisions that are part of the Federal Reserve Act, also distorts the intent of the law. The emergency provisions are aimed at the private sector, including individuals, partnerships, and corporations, and they have always been interpreted as requiring the borrower to demonstrate that he could not obtain adequate credit elsewhere (i.e., from other banking institutions). The spirit of those provisions also would be violated if a deposit insurer or other government agency obtained credit from a commercial bank, which in turn rediscounted the borrower's note with its Federal Reserve Bank. The deposit insurers and some government agencies may be "corporations" as a matter of legal form, but they are federally owned or controlled corporations, and like it or not, that

makes them different. Specifically, it makes them ineligible for Federal Reserve loans without explicit congressional authorization.

Until the last 10 years or so, Federal Reserve, Treasury, and congressional officials generally considered central bank bailouts to aid the Treasury undesirable.[28] In more recent years, however, the Federal Reserve has been aiding the FDIC (and hence the Treasury) by delaying collection of central bank advances to failing institutions.

When the Franklin National Bank failed in 1974, for example, the Federal Reserve postponed for three years collection of its $1.7 billion loan to Franklin to give the FDIC flexibility to conduct an orderly liquidation. Although it postponed repayment, the Fed did not add to the Franklin advance, other than through the accrual of interest, after it became apparent in September 1974 that the bank would fail, nor did the central bank make any new advances to the FDIC after the bank was closed in October. Similarly, when Continental Illinois was rescued in 1984, repayment of $3.5 billion of the Federal Reserve's $8.0 billion advance outstanding on the rescue date was deferred for five years, again to enable the FDIC to conduct an orderly liquidation of Continental's bad assets. As was the case with Franklin, no new advances were made to the bank once it was determined that failure was imminent.

The Fed's loan to Continental matured in September 1989 and was repaid in full—in one final payment of about $2.1 billion. Although the FDIC did not formally request a renewal or extension of the terms of the Continental advance, it did seek one-year forbearances in the Texas bank rescues. The Federal Reserve refrained from collecting $1 billion of its $2.8 billion advance to First Republic, but that advance was repaid in November 1989. Similarly, the Fed did not require immediate repayment of about $1.5 billion of its $1.8 billion advance to MCorp. The FDIC finally repaid the full amount in March 1990. Thus, the FDIC suffered a cash drain of $4.6 billion in order to repay forborne Fed advances in the six-month period between September 1989 and March 1990. Moreover, the prospective cash drain on the FDIC has not diminished. At this writing, press reports indicate that before the onset of the 1990 tax season, which temporarily builds up funding for depository institutions until the Treasury withdraws those balances, the Fed had advances in amounts varying between $1.5 billion and $2.0 billion outstanding to the Bank of New England; those advances have been reduced to less than $500 million since April 15.[29]

Thus, in the absence of a full Treasury guarantee or an explicit act of Congress, or both, neither legal tradition nor precedent establishes a case for the Federal Reserve's funding the deposit insurers or any other federal agency. In a financial crisis, it is the responsibility of the Federal Reserve System to guarantee sufficient aggregate liquidity to the banking system through open-market operations. To go any further in freeing Washington actors to use the central bank to fund insolvent operations that the Treasury is reluctant to underwrite is to court eventual fiscal and monetary disaster.

The arguments for avoiding central bank financing of the Treasury strike some of us as so overwhelming that it seems strange that anyone could object strongly to the traditional views. Any tolerance of central bank financing of the Treasury (other than handing over surplus reserve banks' earnings to the Treasury each year) undermines the principal reason for separating the central bank from the Treasury in the first place: it threatens the nonpolitical nature of monetary policy operations. It makes no logical, legal, or historical sense to establish an independent central bank and then expect it to pay the Treasury's unsecured bills.

As Friedman (1960) noted, laws against counterfeiting are intended to protect the Treasury from loss arising from unauthorized claims. There is no reason to be less on guard against indirect claims on the Treasury or central bank that are created by expanding claims on the deposit insurance funds (or other parts of the safety net) as the result of the actions of private-sector bankers and savings-and-loan executives. The failure of Congress to control or effectively regulate such claims by depository institutions amounts to partial abdication of its constitutional responsibility to maintain political accountability for the expenditure of public moneys.[30]


## Conclusion

There are three positions that could be taken with respect to risk taking by depository institutions: (a) banking powers should not be expanded because of concern about the federal safety net, (b) banking powers should be expanded without retracting some or all of the federal safety net, or (c) banking powers should be expanded *after* the federal safety net issues are addressed. For the purposes of this discussion, expansions of risk-taking powers includes both geographic risk and new investment or asset powers.

Policy position (a) is the only logical and internally consistent position possible for those who both accept the four main propositions discussed above and doubt that Congress and the administration (any administration) will act aggressively to keep separate banks' risk-taking activities and the federal safety net. Historically, foreign experience in that area has been even more depressing than experience in the United States. It appears difficult, even in the best of times, for government officials to keep their hands off and maintain market discipline, especially discipline of large or well-connected institutions.

Such institutions often seem to believe that they have a right to retain all the profits and to share any losses with the taxpayers. When those institutions have their way (as they have in the United States since about 1970),[31] market efficiency loses to central planning and government-sponsored credit allocations. The societal losses are great even if the subsidization scheme seems to work superficially and spares the taxpayers immediate, direct loss. Consequently, proposals that banks give up risk taking as the price of participating in the federal safety net are periodically put forth.[32] Many approaches to insulating the risk-taking activities of depository institutions from the federal safety net have merit, but the real issue was noted by Ely (1989): the political processes in Washington tend to make hash of any good idea for restructuring the financial services industry.

There is reason to be skeptical about our capacity to divorce consideration of the merits of expanded bank powers from concerns about abuse of the federal safety net. The strength of both federal deposit insurance funds has already been undermined by growing numbers of failures of depository institutions; the payment system has been tested (e.g., the Bank of New York computer failure in 1985 and the stock market collapse on October 19, 1987); and the central bank's LLR function is increasingly invoked in Washington as a solution to the dilemmas facing bank and thrift regulators. Thus, policy position (a) is eminently defensible and logical, albeit somewhat unpopular in lobbying circles.

Policy position (b) enjoys a wide array of both industry and official support. Unfortunately that proposal requires a great deal of faith that one's fellow man, in particular Washington politicians, will do the right thing. That position resembles the approach taken by thrift industry regulators in the 1980s—deregulate first and supervise later. The results in the thrift industry were not encouraging. Acceptance of proposal (b) would therefore require that taxpayers forget past problems, including some (e.g., the rising cost of the FSLIC bailout) that should not be forgotten. That approach is currently favored by official Washington and hence has to be regarded as the one most likely to be adopted.

It is not enough for the defenders of policy proposal (b) to say that "we" (it is not always clear who "we" are) can punish the undesirable behavior of those who abuse the federal safety net if only "we" have the will to do so. Financial questions often strike the general public as too complicated to be understood—hence, the widespread delegation of decisionmaking to and reliance on government experts. Meanwhile, those who gain the most from abusing the deposit insurance system strongly resist proposed roll-backs of the safety net or efforts to increase supervision to control risk. Political activity on the part of those who benefit from federal protection may be part of what Ely[33] means by the "tugging by the political processes" that accompanies every reform effort. All the insulation in the world will not prevent those who are intent on abusing the safety net from doing so, nor will it keep those who are so negligent or reckless that they do not recognize the effects of risks on the safety net from abusing it. That is the heart of the moral hazard issue.

To protect the taxpayer, it might be better not to expand banks' risk taking until it becomes clear that the safety net will be retracted as risk taking is expanded. Unfortunately, at the moment there is *no* discussion whatsoever in official Washington of retracting any part of the federal safety net, with or without expansion of bank powers.[34] Most Washington actors limit their discussions to promising increased funds for supervision, regulation, and monitoring the separation of banks' expanded powers from the federal safety net. Well-intended as such measures may be, they are short sighted. Historical experience suggests that political pressures would prevent their working as advertised. Only explicitly reducing the extent of the safety net and limiting politicians' power to expand access to it will succeed. In the present political environment, if a failing bank or thrift institution is sufficiently large or well connected, the monetary and fiscal authorities will try to save it, brushing aside all questions of efficiency and market discipline in the process.

The foregoing analysis of position (b) makes position (c) almost moot. Position (c) requires that we deal with the safety net issues first and then deregulate. However, if it is politically impossible to roll back any part of the federal safety net, then we clearly cannot proceed to the point where it is safe to expand bank powers. Unfortunately, many persons who apparently think they are advocating position (c), an eminently logical, coherent, and defensible proposition, behave or speak as though they are advocating position (b). The crucial difference between (b) and (c) is the order in which reform steps are taken. Deregulating banks first risks a repetition of the FSLIC fiasco of the 1980s.

Banks' risk taking and the federal safety net are closely linked. It is difficult to change one (expanding bank powers) without adversely affecting the other (increasing moral hazard). In centrally planned economies, the risk would be expanded without regard to moral hazard. In the United States we do not intend that result, though we are in danger of achieving it.

The following anecdote may shed some light on the true nature of the present dilemma. A few years ago I had lunch with the general counsel of one of the investment-banking subsidiaries of a large bank holding company. He assured me that the expansion of bank powers would pose no risk to the federal safety net. We recited in unison the dictum that no bank is, or should be, too big to fail. Then I observed that I had yet to hear the following disclaimers from any commercial banker seeking new investment powers:

1.  If I take risks and fail, I will not ask for a bailout.
2.  If a bailout is offered anyway, I will refuse it.
3.  If I am forced to accept the bailout, I will resign rather than take it.

I am still waiting for that banker's disclaimer.

Moreover, although some commercial bankers have threatened to turn in their bank charters if bank powers are not extended, no large commercial bank has actually done so since the 1930s. Yielding its bank charter would seem an excellent way for a well-capitalized institution to expand its corporate powers. However, the only officers of large banks who have approached the Federal Reserve lately about turning in their bank charters have been bank holding company executives who want to walk away from failing subsidiary banks but keep surplus equity within the holding company or in other, solvent bank subsidiaries. Such discussions amount to challenges of the Fed's "bank holding companies as a source of strength" doctrine (Duke 1990) and represent an ill-disguised attempt to get the public to pick up a larger share of the tab for the failing bank.

In the final analysis, most bank officers who talk about giving up their bank charters are reluctant to lose the comparatively cheap funding source provided by federally insured deposits. Insured deposits might not be easy to replace, and funds that commanded a higher return would make it more difficult to continue to hold assets that were worth less than book value. Similarly, continued access to both Fedwire's nearly free guarantees[35] of final payment and below-market-cost funds at the discount window induces bankers to retain their charters. Indeed, those services are also attractive to many "near bankers" and nonbankers trying to gain access to them. As long as a bank charter is the price of admission to cheap funds (insured deposits), Fedwire, and the discount window, as well as a badge that certifies ownership of a franchise with some exclusivity value, a bank charter will have enough value that no officer of a large bank will willingly yield his.

However, policymakers should be able to develop a process whereby solvent bankers who wish to expand their corporate powers immediately could do so. It would take only three steps:

1. Turn in the bank charter.
2. Arrange for insured deposits and other liabilities to be assumed by someone else, to the extent that holders of those liabilities are unwilling to have them held by the ongoing nonbank institution.
3. Turn in the Federal Reserve Bank shares held by all member banks. That move would cut off access to the discount window and Fedwire. Similarly, nonmember depository institutions would give up access to those services by yielding their charters.

Any banker could take those three liberating steps if he were truly willing to reduce his call on the federal safety net and could not wait for Congress to act on expanded bank powers.

Those who advocate plunging ahead with deregulation of risks without first addressing the federal safety net issues are guilty either of naive optimism about the public moneys that are at stake in bank deregulation or of opportunism.

## Epilogue

The Financial Institutions Reform, Recovery and Enforcement Act (FIRREA) of August 9, 1989, was the legislative attempt to deal with many of the issues raised in this paper. The ultimate success or failure of FIRREA should be judged in accordance with the four propositions stated at the beginning of the paper. At this writing (May 1990), it appears that FIRREA is an incomplete solution to the problems inherent in and created by government deposit insurance. Generally accepted estimates of the present value of the FSLIC rescue now are in the range of $125 billion $140 billion, about $1,100 to $1,300 per tax return. The battle against government deposit insurance cannot be considered won until we stop trying to save it, whether its rescue costs are on- or off-budget. The FIRREA scorecard follows.

### No Public Subsidies

The public has taken it on the chin with this one. Everyone, whether rich or poor, is being taxed (or having public debt incurred that is backed by taxing authority) to pay off the liabilities of failed thrift institutions. The arithmetic-mean FSLIC insured deposit account is only about $8,000; the median insured deposit account is somewhat lower (the mean is skewed upward by a small number of large accounts). As the present value of the bailout cost rises, and in a prolonged recession the present-value cost easily could exceed $2,000 per tax return, most individual taxpayers will find it cheaper to walk away from failed thrift institutions, writing off the nonreturn of their nominally insured deposits, than to continue to attempt to pay off failed institutions' liabilities at par value. More than any other legislative proposition in Washington since the entry of the United States into World War I and the flotation of the First Liberty Loan (1917), FIRREA is a bailout of the comparatively rich (and even a few of the extremely rich) financed by taxing the average citizen an amount that approaches or exceeds his entire stake in the game. It is the potlatch theory of economics gone berserk.

Worse yet, the violation of the "no public subsidies" rule may have been fixed in the statute books by FIRREA in a way that will make it impossible to avoid greater costs in the future. Until 1989 only the moral obligation of the United States, expressed in "sense of the Congress" resolutions, guaranteed repayment of insured deposits. Many observers believed that a similar "sense of the Congress" resolution was adopted as part of FIRREA, but on closer inspection of the relevant FIRREA provision [12 U.S.C. §1825(d)], it now appears that all insured deposits accepted on or after August 9, 1989, with stated principal amounts and stated maturity dates, have the explicit full-faith-and-credit backing of the U.S. government. That is probably an unconstitutional delegation to private-sector bankers of the capacity to pledge the credit of the United States or to create binding claims on the Treasury itself. But because no one in Washington seems to care about such constitutional niceties anymore, the ultimate subsidy of the banking system, now worth between $2.5 trillion and $3.0 trillion (roughly one-half of GNP and causing doubling of the publicly held full-faith-and-credit debt of the United States) has gone largely unnoticed and unremarked upon. O tempora, o mores!

## Lender of Last Resort

The LLR supplies liquidity only, not equity or capital replacement. FIRREA, as enacted, observes that principle reasonably well. The FDIC's borrowing authority at the Treasury was increased from $3 billion ($3.75 billion, combined with FSLIC) to $5 billion [apparently available to fund both the Bank Insurance Fund (formerly FDIC) and the Savings Association Insurance Fund (formerly FSLIC)]. The $5 billion may be used in support of expanded FDIC open-bank assistance authority for depository institutions in danger of failing. Unfortunately, in the first large bank crisis since FIRREA was enacted, involving New England banks in early 1990, the Continental Illinois and Texas rescue patterns were recreated, with the Federal Reserve Bank of Boston making multi-month, multi-hundred-millions-of-dollar advances of extended credit. As of this writing, the FDIC has not used its own funds under the expanded lending authority in the New England rescues. Thus, there is a basis for fearing future backsliding.

## Deposit Insurance

Deposit insurance limits should be strictly observed. Unfortunately, FIRREA did not decrease the existing $100,000 deposit insurance limit per insured account. There is some discussion in Washington of reducing the limit, but politically it is quite an unpopular concept. Every dollar of deposit insurance coverage in excess of $10,000 (the current minimum denomination for three-month Treasury bills) is a de facto subsidy of the banking and thrift industries because solvent banks and thrifts ordinarily do not (indeed, in most cases they profitably cannot) offer above-Treasury yields on insured short-term obligations. The ideal government deposit insurance limit remains zero.

## Central Banks

Central banks should not pay the Treasury's bills without being reimbursed. FIRREA did not change the status quo ante in that regard. To the government's credit, $50 billion was appropriated over three years to fund the FSLIC rescue, and a new, separate entity, the Resolution Trust Corporation, was created to oversee the rescue. The rescue funds were not borrowed from the Fed, and the RTC was given no explicit borrowing authority at the Fed. Unfortunately, the RTC keeps nibbling around the edges of a Federal Reserve "working capital" loan as estimated and actual FSLIC rescue costs keep rising. It is reasonable to predict, on the basis of actual experience with the RFC and the Thomas Amendment (Title III) of the Agricultural Adjustment Act of 1933, that nothing short of an explicit statutory prohibition of FDIC or RTC borrowings from the Fed will work in the future to keep the Treasury's hand out of the Fed's pockets. Neither standards nor personalities in Washington are what they used to be, after all.

## Final FIRREA Score

The game is not finished yet, but we're in the last innings, and the classical economic theory pitcher is becoming tired. Only relief in the form of an explicit statutory prohibition of central bank bailout lending and an end to federal deposit insurance could still save the game for taxpayers.

## Notes

1. That is, if Texas savings and loans were given 20 years to liquidate their real estate loan portfolios, and if property values recovered to book value within those 20 years, then Texas S&Ls could be said to have only a "temporary liquidity problem" instead of a rather obvious "solvency" problem.

2. For example, after 1984 bank supervisory authorities treated senior debt of bank holding companies as capital if the weighted average remaining maturity was at least 7 years; mandatorily convertible subordinated debt was treated as capital if the conversion had to occur within 12 years.

3. The U.S. Treasury requires that assets pledged to secure its deposits in the banking system, other than designated classes of government securities and certain permissible investments, mature in not more than two years. The maturity limitation arises for non-marketable obligations because the Treasury must consider both safety and liquidity (ready availability of funds) pertinent factors in the receipt and placement of its funds in the banking system.

4. See, for example, Todd (1988, Appendix C) for a summary of the RFC's solvency (capital) support activities in the 1930s.

5. See Hammond (1957).

6. See Dewey 1903. The prohibition against federal underwriting of general corporate risk was always limited to obvious and large-scale bailouts. Protectionism (a form of preemptive bailout when carried to extremes) and favoritism toward corporations in the courts are as old as the Republic itself. See, for example, Hamilton (1972a, 1972b, 1972c).

7. For more complete descriptions of the RFC's activities, see Penning (1968), Jones (1951), or Upham and Lamke (1934).

8. The FDIC's line of credit with the Treasury amounted to $3 billion before 1989, while the FSLIC was authorized to borrow up to $750 million. Also, in 1982 both the FDIC and the FSLIC were given explicit statutory authority to provide both liquidity and solvency (capital) assistance to open depository institutions under the Garn–St Germain Act. In other words, the federal deposit insurance agencies were granted RFC-like powers that the Federal Reserve does not have under existing statute or precedent. See Todd (1988, Appendix C).

9. On the evils of central planning, whether by the right or the left, see Hayek (1944) and Schumpeter (1950).

10. The temporary deposit insurance fund covered claims arising from bank closings through June 30, 1934.

11. A variation of the original design was revived in the 1980s as the "modified payout plan."

12. Mutual savings banks were also covered by federal deposit insurance for the first time.

13. The RFC's activities during the period were analogous to the virtually unrestricted open-bank assistance powers granted to the FDIC under the Garn–St Germain Act of 1982.

14. It experienced 9 failures in 1934, 25 in 1935, 69 in 1936, 75 in 1937, 74 in 1938, 60 in 1939, and 43 in 1940.

15. See the prophetic warnings of Kane (1985).

16. Bills to reconstitute the RFC do surface periodically. In fact, an unusually large number (six) were filed during the 100th Congress (1987–88).

17. See, for example, McTague and Rehm (1988, p. 3) where Federal Home Loan Bank Board Chairman Danny Wall indicates that one of the options that might be considered for funding the FSLIC is "borrowing funds from . . . the Federal Reserve."

18. See Spero (1980).

19. See Sprague (1986).

20. See Federal Deposit Insurance Corporation (1988, p. 74, Table 129). It is also worth noting the efforts by the FDIC to expand deposit insurance coverage to the entire value of unit trusts that invest in certificates of deposit. The rationale is that such unit trusts are similar to a broker placing deposits that total more than $100,000 for several clients. Because current policy is to view each client's deposit as separate, brokered funds tend to be fully insured. See Rehm (1988).

21. The total deposits of FSLIC-insured S&Ls were $932.8 billion at year-end 1987. Total assets of those institutions were reported at $1,251.7 billion. See Wolf (1988). Most observers assumed that virtually all deposits of FSLIC-insured institutions were insured deposits.

22. FDIC-insured deposits represented 42.9 to 46.8 percent of all deposits in the 1930s, 36.5 to 49.7 percent in the 1940s, 54.1 to 57.4 percent in the 1950s, 55.0 to 63.1 percent in the 1960s, and 60.2 to 76.9 percent in the 1980s.

23. See Caliguire and Thomson (1987).

24. See Sprague (1986, p. 259) and Lever and Huhne (1986, pp. 17–22). It is not clear where the authorities draw the line for "too big to fail." For example, First City had only about $12 billion in assets at its rescue date (September 1987), and First Republic had only about $25 billion in assets at its closing (August 1988). First Republic ranked 14th in the Salomon Brothers listing of U.S. bank holding companies by total assets at year-end 1987. First City would have ranked no higher than 35th at that date.

25. Some writers observe that most failures of depository institutions are due to human failings, not to uncontrollable market forces. See, for example, Heinemann (1988, p. 4).

26. See also Todd (1988).

27. See Hamilton (1972a). It should also be noted that Hamilton was writing under the constraints of the gold standard era, that he would not have advocated loans that might imperil the central bank's solvency, and that his successors as treasury secretary eventually came to understand the evils of central bank funding of the Treasury's accounts. Also, Hamilton's original bank bill limited Treasury borrowings from the First Bank of the United States to $50,000 without explicit congressional authorization. For further discussion of those points, see Todd (1988, Appendix B).

28. The most important exception to that rule was the creation of the FDIC in 1933.

29. See, for example, Board of Governors (1990) and Holland (1990, p. 32).

30. Congress has delegated to the Federal Reserve the power to create claims on the

Treasury by making Federal Reserve notes "obligations of the United States." If reserve banks' advances supporting blanket guarantees of claims on banks are withdrawn in currency, then the delegation described above occurs. Technically, claims on the reserve banks are *not* claims on the United States *unless* the claims are held in the form of currency. Since any advance or reserve account may be withdrawn in currency, all claims on the Federal Reserve Banks may be easily converted into claims on the U.S. Treasury.

31. See Todd (1988).

32. See, for example, Litan (1987) or Federal Reserve Bank of New York (1987).

33. Remarks made during presentation of a paper (Ely 1989).

34. Questions that will need to be addressed explicitly should we ever attempt to reform the safety net include: Should the deposit insurance agencies be retained in anything like their present form? Should they be retained at all? Should the central bank use its LLR function, however defined, to bail out insolvent depository institutions, the deposit insurance agencies, or the Treasury itself? Should the payments mechanism continue to be protected if it has become principally a device for settling trades in the securities and foreign exchange markets with little relationship to payments in the real domestic economy? Such questions are relevant to the discussion but beyond the scope of this particular paper.

35. In 1989 the Federal Reserve implemented a new policy of charging 25 basis points as a penalty for certain types of intraday overdrafts on Fedwire.

## References

Board of Governors of the Federal Reserve System. 1990. "Factors Affecting Reserve Balances of Depository Institutions and Condition Statement of F.R. Banks." Publication H-1. Washington, D.C.: Board of Governors, April 19.

Caliguire, Daria B., and Thomson, James B. 1987. "FDIC Policies for Dealing with Failed and Troubled Institutions." Federal Reserve Bank of Cleveland *Economic Commentary*, October 1.

Dewey, Davis R. 1903. *Financial History of the United States*. New York: Longmans Green & Co.

Duke, Paul, Jr. 1990. "Basis of Fed's Oversight of Bank Firms May Be Questioned in Wake of Ruling." *Wall Street Journal*, May 17, p. A3.

Ely, Bert. 1989. "Technology, Regulation and the Financial Services Industry in the Year 2000." In Federal Reserve Bank of Chicago, *The Financial Services Industry in the Year 2000: Risk and Efficiency*, proceedings of a conference on Bank Structure and Competition, May 11–13, 1988, pp. 578–601.

Federal Deposit Insurance Corporation. 1987. *Annual Report 1986*. Washington, D.C.: FDIC.

Federal Deposit Insurance Corporation. 1988. *Annual Report 1987*. Washington, D.C.: FDIC.

Federal Deposit Insurance Corporation. 1989. *Annual Report 1988*. Washington, D.C.: FDIC.

Federal Reserve Bank of New York. 1987. *Annual Report 1986*.

Friedman, Milton. 1960. *A Program for Monetary Stability*. New York: Fordham University Press.

Hammond, Bray. 1957. *Banks and Politics in America. From the Revolution to the Civil War*. Princeton, N.J.: Princeton University Press.

Hamilton, Alexander. (1904) 1972a. "Opinion as to the Constitutionality of the Bank of the United States" (1791). In *The Works of Alexander Hamilton*, edited by Henry Cabot Lodge, vol. 3, pp. 445–93. Reprint. Brooklyn, N.Y.: Haskell House.

Hamilton, Alexander. (1904) 1972b. "Report on Manufactures" (1791). In *The Works of Alexander Hamilton*, edited by Henry Cabot Lodge, vol. 4, pp. 70–198. Reprint. Brooklyn, N.Y.: Haskell House.

Hamilton, Alexander. (1904) 1972c. "Report on National Bank" (1790). In *The Works of Alexander Hamilton*, edited by Henry Cabot Lodge, vol. 3, pp. 388–443. Reprint. Brooklyn, N.Y.: Haskell House.

Hayek, Friedrich A. 1944. *The Road to Serfdom*. Chicago, Ill.: University of Chicago Press.

Heinemann, H. Erich. 1988. "Pious Phrases Aside, Cause of S&L Crisis Was Fraud, Greed, and Mismanagement." *American Banker*, September 26, pp. 4–5.

Holland, Kelley. 1990. "Bank of New England Said to Be on Mend." *American Banker*, May 18.

Jefferson, Thomas. 1975. "Opinion on the Constitutionality of the National Bank." (1791). In *The Portable Thomas Jefferson*, edited by Merrill D. Peterson, pp. 261–62. New York: Viking Portable Library, no. 80, Penguin Books.

Jones, Jesse H., with Edward Angly. 1951. *Fifty Billion Dollars: My Thirteen Years with the RFC, 1932–1945*. New York: Macmillan.

Kane, Edward J. 1985. *The Gathering Crisis in Federal Deposit Insurance*. Cambridge, Mass.: MIT Press.

Lever, Harold, and Huhne, Christopher. 1986. *Debt and Danger*. Boston: Atlantic Monthly Press.

Litan, Robert E. 1987. *What Should Banks Do?* Washington, D.C.: Brookings Institution.

McTague, Jim, and Rehm, Barbara. 1988. "Wall Now Says FSLIC Needs $45 Billion." *American Banker*, October 6, p. 3.

Penning, Ann Cooper. 1968. "Aid to Distressed Banks—Yesterday and Today." Graduate School of Banking dissertation. Rutgers University.

Rehm, Barbara. 1988. "FDIC Proposes Extended Coverage." *American Banker*, October 12, p. 3.

Schumpeter, Joseph A. 1950. *Capitalism, Socialism and Democracy*. 3d ed. New York: Harper & Row.

Spero, Joan Edelman. (1942) 1980. *The Failure of the Franklin National Bank*. New York: Columbia University Press.

Sprague, Irvine. 1986. *Bailout*. New York: Basic Books.

Todd, Walker F. 1988. "Lessons of the Past and Prospects for the Future in Lender of Last Resort Theory." Federal Reserve Bank of Cleveland Working Paper no. 8805, August.

Upham, Cyril B., and Lamke, Edwin. 1934. *Closed and Distressed Banks: A Study in Public Administration*. Washington, D.C.: Brookings Institution.

Wolf, Frederick D. 1988. "The Federal Savings and Loan Insurance Corporation—Current Financial Condition and Outlook." Statement before the Senate Committee on Banking, Housing, and Urban Affairs, May 19.

# COMMENT ON INSULATING BANKS

## John H. Kareken

In his paper James Pierce argues, relying to an extent on Chase, Laub and Company (1987), that the banks of any bank holding company can be insulated from the losses experienced by or even the failure of one of the holding company's nonbank subsidiaries. That is to say, the losses or the failure of a nonbank subsidiary need have no direct effect on the holding company's banks. Pierce also argues that all holding company banks should be insulated and, moreover, that once they have been, all nonbank subsidiaries should be entirely deregulated. He means something particular, though, by "insulated" and therefore by "bank." If holding company banks are ever insulated in the way Pierce advocates, they will differ greatly, especially in the services they offer, from the holding company banks of the present.

## Federal Reserve Opposition

The Federal Reserve System, responsible for regulating all bank holding companies, has long maintained that insulating holding company banks is

The author is Minnesota Professor of Banking and Finance in the Carlson School of Management, University of Minnesota.

impossible. And, indeed, it may not matter at all that a holding company bank has had no financial dealings with any of the nonbank affiliates of the holding company. As long as holding company banks hold risky assets, the financial difficulties of a nonbank affiliate of a holding company may cause lenders to lose confidence in its banks. But as Pierce argues, a fleeting liquidity crisis is not something that need worry the Federal Reserve. It can make a discount window loan of whatever amount to any bank that has momentarily lost the confidence of lenders.

For Pierce, the second of the Federal Reserve's two traditional arguments is not convincing either. To save its good name, a holding company bank may well want to do whatever is required to help a nonbank affiliate that has encountered serious financial problems. As Pierce observes, though, that a holding company bank may want to help a sister nonbank affiliate does not make insulation impossible. The current law, if enforced, can keep the bank from attempting a rescue. That law seems inadequate, but that is, as Pierce maintains, because the Federal Reserve has never been convincing about its willingness to be a vigorous enough enforcer. Pierce would have the Federal Reserve seek jail sentences for the chief executive officers and directors of the parent holding companies and of the banks that have violated the law. That is not something that the system has ever done.

## The Need for Deregulation

It is easy to accept Pierce's contention that the Federal Reserve has been wrong in opposing a policy of deliberately insulating holding company banks. No one should expect, though—certainly Pierce does not—that the system will soon do a flip-flop, or declare publicly for insulating holding company banks and, what would seem to be a corollary, complete deregulation of the nonbank subsidiaries of holding companies.

Pierce views holding company (corporate) structure as endogenous, determined in part by the regulatory regime. His analysis, a tour de force, leads him to an important conclusion. The FDIC has confirmed by deed that it has abandoned its policy, evident in the Continental Illinois rescue, of keeping holding company and nonbank subsidiary creditors from losing money. And the Federal Reserve continues to regulate the nonbank subsidiaries of holding companies as if they were holding company banks. The incentive is therefore for holding companies to locate activities that involve funding in their banks or the subsidiaries thereof. If the holding companies are allowed to continue locating those activities there, then when the Glass-Steagall Act has at long last been rendered meaningless, they will borrow through their banks at the risk-free rate to support their investment-banking activities. If that prospect is frightening, Pierce argues that holding companies will not be able to compete effectively if they are forced to locate nonbank activities, whatever they may be, in nonbank subsidiaries. Such is the burden of Federal Reserve regulation of those subsidiaries.

## How to Define "Bank"

For Pierce, deregulation of nonbank subsidiaries of holding companies is the only real option. There can, however, be no deregulation until after it has been decided what bank holding companies and banks are to be allowed to do. Pierce would limit banks to serving as payment agents for owners of transaction accounts; doing daily settlements; and, surprisingly, making low-risk, easily liquidated loans. But if newly defined banks are to be lenders, even to the least risky of borrowers, it will presumably be necessary for the federal government to go on insuring deposit owners and examining banks, despite the evidence that bank's examination conducted by federal regulatory agencies are frequently worthless. Arguably, it would be better (Kareken 1985) to require newly defined banks to hold only Treasury securities, with market value always equal to deposit liabilities, and, there being no more risk of bank failure, to close up the FDIC.

Pierce claims, but without providing a supporting argument, that forcing banks to hold only Treasury securities would "reduce and distort the provision of credit to private borrowers." That is extremely doubtful, if only because in the bright new world of tomorrow any holding company would be able to have not only newly defined banks but also any number of unregulated lending subsidiaries. Then too, if forcing banks to hold only Treasury securities would do as Pierce alleges, forcing them to make only low-risk, easily liquidated loans could also. Economic efficiency may require that banks as lenders be restricted no more than they are at present.

An empirical observation would seem to be of relevance here: in a dim past banks emerged as, and they have remained, intermediaries, borrowing from and making loans to all manner of companies and individuals. That has to give pause, for to date no one has satisfactorily explained why banks, although the classic intermediaries, have also long served as payment agents. That they have done so may be no more than a historical accident that with the help of government became a tradition. If in a dim past there were only what are called banks, then banks would have ended up doing all that customers wanted done. It is most regrettable, but until banks as intermediaries and payment agents have been convincingly explained, no proposal for making transaction or checking accounts safe (or, for Pierce, nearly safe) by imposing portfolio restrictions on the keepers of those accounts can be readily embraced.

## References

Chase, Laub & Company. 1987. "Insulating Banks from Risks Run by Nonbank Affiliates." Paper prepared for the American Bankers Association, Washington, D. C., October.

Kareken, John. 1985. "Ensuring Financial Stability." In *The Search for Financial Stability: The Past Fifty Years*, pp. 53–75. Federal Reserve Bank of San Francisco.

# COMMENT ON BANK INSULATION

Gerald P. O'Driscoll, Jr.

As a discussant, I find myself in the awkward position of being in substantial agreement with both Pierce and Todd. My position is awkward because the two papers come to nearly opposite conclusions about bank insulation. James Pierce's assessment is that bank insulation cannot become a practical reality until the Federal Reserve is taken out of the business of regulating nonbank affiliates. In contrast, Walker Todd concludes that those who advocate additional deregulation without first addressing the safety net problem can be charged either with excessive optimism or with opportunism.

I am drawn, of course, not to the papers' conclusions but to their diagnoses and analyses. I am especially attracted to the diagnoses and analyses of the safety and soundness issues raised by the current regulatory framework. I am less concerned about where the authors come down on

The author is vice president and associate director of research at the Federal Reserve Bank of Dallas. His comments reflect only his own opinion; they do not represent the official position of any part of the Federal Reserve System.

the issues in the end, because I believe that before we can rationally discuss policy, we need to agree on the nature of the problem.

Pierce and Todd clearly and correctly identify the problem. First, as Pierce observes, the federal safety net is the linchpin of bank insulation. Todd's paper is even more centrally focused on how the safety net mechanism, including its administration, has shaped the current problems in banking. In that context, deposit insurance is the most important of the financial safety nets. The system has created a colossal moral hazard problem. By insuring 100 percent of deposits up to at least $100,000, the insurance agencies have made depositors substantially indifferent to the quality of the portfolios of the depository institutions in which they place their money. In fact, a headline in the November 2, 1988, *Wall Street Journal* reflected just that point: "Shaky Banks and Thrifts Are Solid Bet for Grabbing High Yields" (Peers 1988). It is also true, as the article observes at the end, that "there is an ethical issue in all this. People who pick a certificate of deposit (CD) without regard to safety are ultimately counting on their fellow taxpayers to make good on their high flying expectations if their bank does go bust."

Insolvent depository institutions' bidding for funds is, as Kane (1985, p. 159) has so appropriately put it, a Ponzi scheme. As Todd observes, it also amounts to allowing private persons to create binding claims on the Treasury. Todd's paper also focuses on another element of the financial safety net, namely the lender-of-last-resort facility, now lodged in the Federal Reserve System, the U.S. central bank. The facility has great potential for both good and evil. Todd's paper focuses on the potential harm if the lender-of-last-resort facility is abused, and he identifies its proper role: lending to support short-term liquidity needs of depository institutions, not engaging in equity investment for capital replenishment. The statement could have been written by Walter Bagehot. It is classic central bank doctrine, and I wholeheartedly concur with it. In addition, Todd's recounting of how far we have already strayed from the ideal is disheartening. More to the point are the questions raised by any suggestion of the Fed's lending directly to the deposit insurance funds as a subterfuge to avoid a taxpayer bailout. Among many other things, that would politicize the monetary policy process. Moreover, if done once for one purpose, I do not see how it would be stopped, and every purpose then would be knocking at the door. We would be on the slippery slope of subordinating the conduct of monetary policy to the financing of Treasury obligations. I think there is ample evidence of the harm that could bring.

I am going to return to Todd's paper in a moment, but I want to go back briefly to Pierce's paper and focus on a fundamental issue that he raises: is insulation desirable? Pierce correctly points out that insulation cuts two ways. By insulating banks from both the variance and returns associated with the operations of nonbank subsidiaries, public policy not only protects the banks from losses but it also deprives them of profits. A good case can be made for expanding the types of assets that banks are permitted to hold. The public discussion of risk often misses a very important point. The desirability of even a conservatively managed institution's buying a particular asset or engaging in a particular activity does not depend on the variance in returns on (i.e., the risk inherent in) that asset or activity. What matters is how acquiring that asset or engaging in that activity affects the institution's overall riskiness—that is the variance in returns for the whole portfolio of assets. It is standard material in finance theory courses to explain how a particular asset with a high variance (risk) but a low covariance with the returns on other assets can reduce rather than enhance the risk of a portfolio. Those considerations suggest that policymakers need to turn the bank examination process on its head. Instead of being taught to worry about what they find in a bank's portfolio, examiners should be taught to worry about what they do not find. Next to capital, diversification is the most important protection against bank insolvency.

The case for permitting greater diversification of bank portfolios stands regardless of what is done to reform deposit insurance. I realize that is a controversial proposition. In defense, I can only briefly summarize the argument I have made elsewhere (O'Driscoll 1988a, 1988b). First of all, as Todd reminds us, there are two basic parts to the Glass-Steagall Act. The first is the limitation on bank powers and the second, added almost as an afterthought, is deposit insurance. In my view, the limitation on bank powers does not, as frequently has been argued, offset perverse incentives of deposit insurance (Kareken 1983). In fact, the limitation on bank powers reinforces the incentives to take excessive risk. It reinforces them by preventing banks from reducing overall risk through diversification.

Having made that point, I will conclude by offering an overall assessment of the two papers. It seems to me that, despite having been written from within the Federal Reserve System, Todd's paper is ultimately the more radical of the two. First, he takes a classical or strict view of the lender of last resort. The lender of last resort does not lend to bail out individual institutions but provides liquidity support to the banking system as a whole. Second, given that view and other legal issues that Todd raises, there should be no direct lending to the deposit insurance funds. As a corollary, Congress then must conduct any bailout of the deposit insurance funds. The clear implication of that position is that, faced with congressional inaction, the Fed should allow deposit insurance agencies to

go bankrupt rather than lend to them. That leaves the problem squarely up
to Congress to resolve.

## References

Kane, Edward. 1985. *The Gathering Crisis in Federal Deposit Insurance*. Cambridge,
  Mass.: MIT Press.
Kareken, John H. 1983. "The First Step in Bank Deregulation: What about the
  FDIC?" *American Economic Review* 73 (May): 198–203.
O'Driscoll, Gerald P., Jr. 1988a. "Deposit Insurance in Theory and Practice." *Cato
  Journal* 7 (Winter): 661–75.
O'Driscoll, Gerald P., Jr. 1988b. "Bank Failures: The Deposit Insurance Con-
  nection." *Contemporary Policy Issues* 6 (April): 1–12.
Peers, Alexandra. 1988. "Shaky Banks and Thrifts Are Solid Bet for Grabbing
  Yields." *Wall Street Journal*, November 2, pp. C1, C11.

# IV PAYMENT SYSTEM RISK

# 7 DAYLIGHT OVERDRAFTS: WHO REALLY BEARS THE RISK?

Robert T. Clair

Numerous governmental and private-sector studies have addressed the problem of payment system risk in recent years.[1] The consensus emerging from those studies is that daylight overdrafts are the primary source of risk in the U.S. electronic payment systems. The institutions that create overdrafts do not bear the full costs, and although recent regulation of the large-dollar transfer systems has reduced somewhat the risk associated with overdrafts, problems remain.

Policymakers are also concerned that programs designed to limit risk may interfere with the ability of the payment systems to efficiently carry out transactions. Instituting rigid controls on overdrafts could reduce real economic growth. In attempting to balance the risk posed by daylight overdrafts and the need to expeditiously execute payments, most economists favor attaching an explicit price to overdrafts, thus requiring the institutions that create them to internalize some of the associated

The author is a senior economist with the Federal Reserve Bank of Dallas. The opinions expressed are those of the author and do not necessarily reflect the opinions of the Federal Reserve Bank of Dallas or the Board of Governors of the Federal Reserve System.

117

costs. Such a policy would discourage the use of daylight overdrafts and concomitantly reduce the risk to the payment system.

Although it is widely accepted that there is significant payment system risk, the magnitude of that risk is unknown. Current measures of risk are inadequate and incomplete. Furthermore, few analysts have stopped to determine who actually bears the risk. I suggest that the risk associated with daylight overdrafts is borne at least partially by the taxpaying public. Pricing the extension of intraday credit would be an excellent approach to limiting risk; however, a market-determined price for such credit is more likely to properly allocate the risk than is a government-determined price. Federal Reserve pricing of daylight overdrafts would be an improvement on the current situation, but it would offer only a second-best solution.

## The Current Payment Systems

### Background

Specialized payment systems for large sums have developed in response to the demands of transactors. Those specialized systems differ from normal check-clearing payment systems in three ways: security, speed, and finality. Because transactors value increased security when making extremely large payments, they use systems that have tight safeguards against accidental loss or theft. Similarly, the value of increasing the speed with which a payment is completed is proportionate to its size. The cost of float can be most effectively reduced by speeding the processing of the largest payments. Finally, transactors place great value on finality when the payments are extremely large. Most large-dollar payment systems either provide final payment at the time of the transaction or attempt to minimize the time until the final transfer of funds is completed (Humphrey 1984).

Large-dollar payment systems are conduits for transferring funds between buyers and sellers. As many as five entities may be involved in large-dollar payments: the sender, the sending bank, the transfer system, the receiving bank, and the receiver. The sender is the person or corporation that wishes to transfer funds to a receiver, another individual or corporation, usually in payment for goods, services, or securities received. The sender notifies its bank, known as the sending bank, to debit the sender's account and transfer the funds to the receiver. The sending bank notifies the transfer system to debit the sending bank's account, to credit the receiving bank's account, and to pass the payment information on to the receiving bank. The receiving bank then credits the receiver's account and notifies the receiver of the transfer.[2]

## Large-Dollar Payment Systems

There are two important large-dollar payment systems in the United States, Fedwire and the Clearing House Interbank Payment System. Fedwire is operated by the Federal Reserve System and has existed in various forms since 1918. Fedwire large-dollar transactions comprise funds transfers and book-entry securities transfers. The average daily volume on Fedwire in the second quarter of 1988 was $605 billion in funds transfers and an additional $358 billion in book-entry securities transfers. Average daily payment volume is plotted in Figure 7-1 (based on data from the Division of Research and Statistics of the Federal Reserve System, September 1988). Fedwire conducts an average of 55 million transactions per year and serves 11,000 participating institutions.[3] A study by the Federal Reserve Bank of New York (1987–88) revealed that transfers on Fedwire involve primarily federal funds (33.5 percent of the total dollars transferred), securities transactions (27.8 percent of the total), and commercial and miscellaneous payments (17.0 percent of the total).

Fedwire is the only provider of gross settlement services in the United States. In a gross settlement system, funds are actually transferred when the transfer message is sent. Gross settlement on Fedwire requires the reserve accounts at the Federal Reserve Banks to be credited or debited at the time of the transfer, though the debiting can create a negative balance in a reserve account. That approach provides settlement finality; that is, transferred funds are irrevocably credited to receivers. Once the transfer has been completed, the Fed has no recourse to the receiver to reclaim the funds. The Fed's only recourse is to the sending bank.

The other major large-dollar payment system is the New York Clearing House Association's Clearing House Interbank Payment System, which was formed in 1970. Originally, CHIPS was intended to handle international transactions, which still make up the majority of its business, but it now also handles domestic transactions. CHIPS had an average daily volume of $635 billion in the second quarter of 1988 and served approximately 140 banks (see Figure 7-1). There is relatively little overlap between CHIPS and Fedwire. CHIPS is still used primarily for international transactions; it handles 99 percent of the foreign exchange market and 75 percent of the Eurodollar placement market. Those two markets account for 82 percent of the total dollar volume transferred on CHIPS.

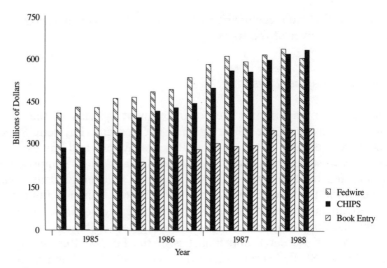

Figure 7–1.   Average Daily Volume of Payments

CHIPS uses net settlement (Mengle 1985). Net settlement differs from gross settlement in that the actual transfer of funds occurs only once a day, which greatly reduces the number of transfers that must be made to complete payments. The single payment needed for settlement is calculated as the sum of all payments sent less the sum of all payments received. Banks whose payments sent exceed payments received are said to be in a net debit position. Such institutions make a single payment through Fedwire to the CHIPS settlement account at the end of the day. After those payments have been made, funds are transferred through Fedwire to CHIPS participants whose payments received exceed payments sent, that is, banks in a net credit position.

## Risk within the Payment Systems

Payment system risk for Fedwire results from the extension of intraday credit through daylight overdrafts. A daylight overdraft occurs whenever a sending bank sends more funds than it currently has in its reserve account (i.e., the sending bank's reserve account has a negative balance). Fedwire treats the transfer of funds as final for the receiving bank and stipulates that the sending bank must have sufficient funds to cover its reserve account at the end of the day. The Fed does have the right to refuse to conduct a transfer if it has reason to believe that the transfer will create an overdraft that cannot be covered by day's end. Under normal circumstances, however, the Fed does not exercise that right. If a bank with an overdraft were to fail during the day, the Fed would be an unsecured creditor and would face a possible loss.

The Federal Reserve permits daylight overdrafts because it believes that the use of intraday credit leads to a more efficient payment mechanism. In its report, the Task Force on Controlling Payment System Risk (1988a) stated that intraday credit allows payments to be completed more quickly and at a lower cost than would otherwise be the case. The task force also recognized that extending intraday credit is costly, especially in terms of risk. It concluded that a careful analysis of the costs and benefits is needed to determine the amount of intraday credit that is optimal for the economy.[4]

Before 1991 the Federal Reserve treated overdrafts that resulted from book-entry securities transactions differently than it did those that occurred in funds transfers. In particular, the Fed did not apply its risk reduction programs to overdrafts created by book-entry securities transactions. The Fed was concerned about any regulation of the government securities market that might interfere with its execution of monetary policy. Furthermore, arguments were made that those transactions were secured by the value of the government securities and consequently were not risky. In the case of book-entry securities transactions, the social gain from providing intraday credit was thought to exceed the social costs. Beginning in early 1991, however, the Fed required that overdrafts resulting from book-entry securities transactions be included in the calculation of total overdrafts. Since the analysis in this chapter is based on 1988 data, all references to Fedwire will pertain only to the funds transfer component unless specifically noted.

Overdrafts are possible on a gross settlement system but not on a net settlement system such as CHIPS. Daylight overdrafts, in a strict sense, do not occur in the CHIPS system because the payment messages transferred by CHIPS represent payment information and obligations to transfer the funds required to settle the payment at the end of the day. Consequently, the receiving bank is a creditor of the sending bank during the day (i.e., it extends intraday credit to the sending bank). The attendant risk is exacerbated by the common practice of permitting receiving customers access to the provisional funds before final settlement. Such access to provisional funds might put the receiving bank in the position of having to settle its CHIPS account before it could retrieve the funds it had advanced to its customer.

The two most important risks in any payment system are settlement risk and systemic risk. Settlement risk is the risk that an institution will be unable to make its settlement (i.e., it will not have sufficient funds to pay what it owes its creditors).[5] In the event of a settlement failure, the bearer of the loss is determined by the type of settlement used by the payment system. In a gross settlement payment system that permits overdrafts, such as Fedwire, the payment system itself bears the risk. The funds are finally and irrevocably credited to the receiver. The payment system could lose the amount of the outstanding overdraft of the failed institution.[6]

A payment system that uses net settlement has specific rules for dealing with a settlement failure. On CHIPS the obligations of the sending banks are irrevocable; a settlement failure does not eliminate the obligation of the sending bank. But the transfers of funds are considered provisional until settlement is made.

If an institution failed to make settlement on the CHIPS system, CHIPS would "unwind" the failing institution's transactions and recalculate settlement entries for all remaining participants. An unwind requires that all transactions with the failed bank on that day be separated from the day's other transactions and that net settlement positions for other institutions be recalculated. As a result of the recalculation, some banks that had previously been able to settle might no longer be able to do so if their successful settlement depended on receiving payments owed them by the failed bank. If the change in the net settlement position of those banks were larger than their capital, they might fail as well. If one or more additional CHIPS participants were unable to settle, then CHIPS would again unwind transactions involving the newly insolvent banks and recalculate settlement. The unwinds and recalculations would continue until all remaining banks could settle their accounts.

The settlement failure of one CHIPS participant can result in the failure of other participants. The risk of multiple related failures is known as systemic risk.[7] Although there has never been a settlement failure on CHIPS, one simulation of an extreme failure indicated that potentially one-third of all participants might fail as the result of a single settlement failure (Humphrey 1986).

To better control that risk, CHIPS has adopted a program for settlement finality based on the use of collateralized funds to cover the settlement obligations of any CHIPS participant that is unable to settle at the end of the day. The program, which is expected to be in effect by late 1990, is referred to as the Additional Settlement Obligation. The settlement finality program will require remaining participants to make up the shortfall of funds needed to settle in proportion to the credit limits each participant has extended to the participant failing to settle. Those funds will be used to strike a settlement but will not remove the obligation of the participant that has failed to settle to properly discharge its obligations (Clair, forthcoming).

To ensure that sufficient liquidity exists to complete settlement, CHIPS participants will be required to hold collateral in the form of either federal funds or U.S. Treasury securities. The collateral required for an individual institution is designed to be sufficient to fund settlement should any one CHIPS participant fail, and the collateral may be sufficient to fund a settlement even if several small participants fail. The Federal Reserve Bank of New York will act as the custodian of the collateral.

The loss-sharing arrangement and collateralization eliminate the systemic risk in the payment system that could result from a single failure. Under the loss-sharing arrangement, a single failure will not cause multiple failures on the payment system. Only multiple unexpected failures that occur in the same day and are unrelated to payment system exposure could result in a situation in which the collateral might be insufficient to complete settlement.

## Policy Concerns

Payment system risk gives rise to two major policy concerns. First, a settlement failure on CHIPS presently could result in a systemic problem if several institutions failed. Second, a settlement failure on Fedwire could cause a substantial loss to the Federal Reserve. Systemic risk and multiple failures could shock the payment system so severely that the ability to make large-dollar payments would be disrupted. In that event, the real growth rate of the economy could be reduced.

The level of risk is dependent on two factors: the size of the loss in the event of a settlement failure and the probability of the unexpected failure of a participant. The dollar amount of daylight overdrafts, and therefore the potential loss, is staggering (see Figure 7-2, which is based on data from the Division of Research and Statistics of the Federal Reserve Board, September 1988). Average daily daylight overdrafts on Fedwire in September 1988 were roughly $55 billion, and earlier in the year overdrafts had been as high as $65 billion. Net debit positions on the CHIPS system were $45 billion in September 1988, relatively close to their high for the year of nearly $48 billion.

Total overdrafts are not necessarily an accurate measure of the risk exposure of the payment system or of the Fed's probable loss in the event of a failure, however. If a single failure were to occur on Fedwire, the Fed's losses could be at most equal to the largest overdraft of the failed

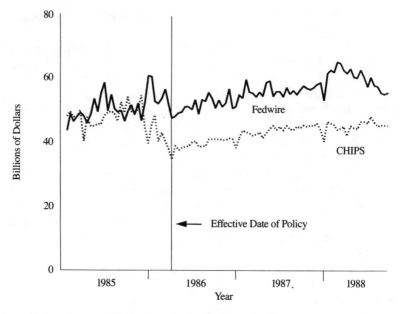

Figure 7–2.   Average Daily Overdrafts, by Transfer System

institution.[8] Unfortunately, the daylight overdrafts of individual institutions are not published, but they clearly are not evenly split among the 1,100 participants that typically incur them. As might be expected, the large U.S. banks account for a disproportionate share of the funds overdrafts on Fedwire and CHIPS. As shown in Figure 7–3 (based on data from the Division of Research and Statistics of the Federal Reserve System, September 1988), large U.S. banks (total assets in excess of $10 billion) accounted for over 40 percent of overdrafts in September 1988. The average daily overdraft of a large institution was $911 million. Therefore, it is fully possible for the Fed to face a loss of $1 billion in the event of a single participant's failure.

The risk calculus of the payment system is dependent not only on the amount of the daylight overdrafts, or the net debit positions, but also on the risk of a bank's failing to settle. A failure has to be unexpected for it to have an effect on settlement. Banks that are known to be in danger of failing are monitored very closely by the Federal Reserve to prevent them from being in an overdraft position. A bank's financial condition before failure usually deteriorates slowly. Because it can takes weeks, months, or even years for a bank to finally fail, it is hard to conceive of a set of

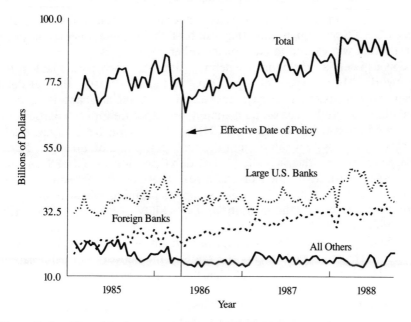

Figure 7–3.   Biweekly Average Amounts of Overdrafts

circumstances that would result in a totally unexpected failure. The sudden discovery of embezzlement or massive fraud has been suggested, but fraud of that magnitude is hard to imagine.[9]

Simulations of settlement failures offer evidence that if a settlement failure were to occur on CHIPS, the systemic failure of other participants would be probable. Furthermore, the number of endangered CHIPS participants and the dollar volume of their electronic funds transfers might create a serious problem. The simulations raise questions about the ability of the payment mechanism to carry out its function. Even though settlement failure on Fedwire would not entail systemic risk, the Fed could incur a substantial loss.

## Current Policies for Reducing Risks

Current policies for reducing risks in the payment system impose several limits or caps on the size of overdrafts, or net debit positions, individual banks can incur when transferring funds. The Federal Reserve has required CHIPS to establish bilateral net credit limits and a network cap on the overall net debit position. The bilateral net credit limits are set by each CHIPS participant, and they establish the maximum net credit every institution will extend to each of the other participants. The network net debit cap sets a maximum net debit position for each participant in the network.[10] In the event of a participant's failing to settle, the net debit cap limits the loss that the payment system as a whole must absorb, and the bilateral net credit caps set a maximum loss exposure for each participant.

In addition to those limits on CHIPS, the Federal Reserve has established a cross-system cap to limit the total daylight debit position of each participant (i.e., the sum of the net debit position on CHIPS and the daylight overdraft position on Fedwire). The cross-system cap is a multiple of the depository institution's capital position, which is based on a self-assessment by the institution of its ability to manage the payment system risk.

Finally, the Fed imposes a cap on daylight overdrafts on the Fedwire system. That cap is essentially the same as the network net debit cap on the CHIPS system. The Fed calculates the cap as the cross-system cap less the net debit position on CHIPS.[11]

Thus, there are essentially four caps: There are two network net debit caps, one for Fedwire and one for CHIPS, that limit the exposure of the payment systems to risk as the result of any one institution's use of intraday credit. There is also a cross-system cap that limits the exposure of the combined payment systems to risk due to any one institution's use of intraday credit. Finally, there are bilateral net credit limits designed to limit systemic risk by restricting the exposure of each individual institution to risk attributable to the intraday credit use of other participants in CHIPS. A bilateral credit limit is not needed in the Fedwire system because gross settlement involves no systemic risk.

## Enforcement of the Caps

CHIPS is currently more advanced than is Fedwire in monitoring compliance with the caps and thereby limiting risk exposure. CHIPS monitors net debit positions on a real-time basis. Any attempt to send through CHIPS a transfer that would violate either a net debit cap or a bilateral credit limit is rejected. Fedwire, in contrast, monitors only a few select institutions on a real-time basis and the majority of banks on an ex post basis.[12] Thus, the Fed honors all funds transfer requests from institutions monitored on an ex post basis, even those that exceed the overdraft limits. It is only after the fact that the Fed counsels a bank on its excessive use of daylight overdrafts. The limitations of ex post monitoring are particularly troublesome given the premise that the greatest risk to the payment system would result from an unexpected failure. Ex post monitoring would provide no useful information on the day an institution was building a large daylight overdraft and unexpectedly failed.

Daylight overdrafts that result from the transfer of book-entry securities on Fedwire are not only included (since 1991) in total overdrafts, they are restricted in other ways. The greatest risk occurs when a securities dealer is attempting to "build a position" to fill an order for a large block of securities. Before January 1988, securities dealers were not permitted to deliver partial orders, so they were required to build their entire position before transfer to the final recipient was made. As a result, a dealer would acquire securities throughout the day, and each transaction would increase his daylight overdraft. At the end of the day, the dealer would deliver the large block of securities and receive payment that covered his overdraft position. To limit that type of daylight overdraft, the Federal Reserve has now restricted the maximum size of a securities transfer to $50 million, which effectively mandates partial delivery of large orders. As a result, securities dealers can now make several partial deliveries during the day and receive partial payments that reduce their daylight overdrafts.[13]

## Efficacy of Risk Reduction Policies

Before the efficacy of the risk reduction policies can be determined empirically, the date of their implementation needs to be established. The effective date of the caps on overdrafts and net debit positions is not clear. The Fed required all private networks that used its net settlement service to implement bilateral credit limits and network net debit caps by March 1986 (Belton et al. 1987). The cross-system cap was also to go into effect at that time.

However, the private sector implemented the Federal Reserve's risk reduction program long before the mandated date. CHIPS established bilateral credit caps in October 1984. One year later, and five months before the board required it, CHIPS implemented a network net debit cap.

A simple measure of effectiveness is the reduction in overdrafts that occurred after the implementation of the caps. Table 7-1 gives the average amount of overdrafts on each transfer system before and after the date of implementation.[14] There was a substantial reduction of $7.3 billion in average daily overdrafts, a 15.4 percent decline, on the CHIPS network after the imposition of net debit caps. But after the March 1986 imposition

Table 7–1.  Average Overdrafts (Billions of Dollars)

|                                | CHIPS | Fedwire (Funds Only) |
|--------------------------------|-------|----------------------|
| Implementation date            |       |                      |
| October 1985                   |       |                      |
| Three quarters before          | 47.3  | 46.8                 |
| Three quarters after           | 40.0  | 49.5                 |
| Change                         | −7.3  | 2.7                  |
| March 1986                     |       |                      |
| Three quarters before          | 47.7  | 48.5                 |
| Three quarters after           | 39.5  | 49.1                 |
| Change                         | −8.2  | 0.6                  |
| Last three quarters            | 44.7  | 57.9                 |
| Change from average for three  |       |                      |
| quarters before March 1986     | −3.0  | 9.4                  |

*Source:* Board of Governors of the Federal Reserve System, Division of Research and Statistics, September 1988.

of Fedwire and cross-system caps, daylight overdrafts did not decline on Fedwire.

It appears that the caps have not substantially reduced overdrafts on the Fedwire system, but they may have had an effect on the CHIPS system. The implementation dates are sufficiently close to make it difficult to attribute the decline in CHIPS overdrafts to either its implementation of net debit caps or the Fed's implementation of overdraft caps and cross-system caps. Comparison of overdrafts before and after the Fed's implementation of caps indicates that overdrafts were not reduced on Fedwire; they were $9.4 billion higher in November 1988 than before the introduction of caps. Overdrafts on CHIPS were less in late 1988 than they were before March 1986, but they were growing.

Caps have had relatively little effect on overdrafts because the current caps are too high to constrain most participants. Table 7–2 gives the aggregate cap usage rate expressed as the total of overdrafts on CHIPS and Fedwire (funds only) as a percentage of the total permissible overdraft (i.e., the cross-system cap) as of the two weeks ending September 21, 1988. Small domestic banks used relatively little of their allowable overdrafts, only 19.6 percent, and large domestic banks with over $10 billion in assets used only 40.5 percent of their permitted intraday credit. If the cap is not binding, the marginal cost of incurring additional overdrafts is near zero. It is no wonder that overdrafts did not decline on Fedwire. Moreover, the

Table 7–2.   Distribution of Aggregate Funds Overdrafts and Cap Usage Rates

| Type of Institution | Number of Institutions | Percentage of Total Funds Overdrafts | Aggregate Cap Usage Rate (Percent) |
|---|---|---|---|
| Domestic, by asset size (billions of dollars) | | | |
| Less than 1 | 2,066 | 6.5 | 19.6 |
| 1–5 | 189 | 6.2 | 17.3 |
| 5–10 | 49 | 7.0 | 22.5 |
| More than 10 | 41 | 43.6 | 40.5 |
| Foreign[a] | 94 | 36.7 | 10.4 |
| All | 2,439 | 100.0 | 17.8 |

Source: Board of Governors of the Federal Reserve System, Division of Research and Statistics, September 1988.

Note: For the two weeks ending September 21, 1988, total funds overdraft capacity was $481.5 billion and actual funds overdrafts were $85.7 billion. Institutions with negative adjusted primary capital or zero or no caps on file are excluded. Such institutions accounted for about 0.1 percent of cross-system overdrafts.

[a] U.S. branches and agencies of foreign banks. The cross-system overdraft capacity of those institutions is based on worldwide capital. However, their uncollateralized Fedwire capacity is based on the smaller measure of 5 percent of their U.S. third-party liabilities.

overdraft usage rates given in Table 7–2 are based on current caps that are lower than those imposed in March 1986. Caps were reduced on January 14, 1988, and again on May 19, 1988.

CHIPS caps appear to have been more effective than Fedwire caps in reducing daylight overdrafts. CHIPS does not publish data similar to those available from Fedwire, but CHIPS caps are much lower than the cross-system caps imposed by Fedwire. Consequently, CHIPS caps may have been binding for many participants and may have reduced overdrafts. It is possible that the binding constraint of CHIPS caps encouraged use of Fedwire on which caps are not binding.

The gross amount of overdrafts may be rising, but it does appear that the growth rate of overdrafts has slowed relative to the growth rate of payments. Overdrafts per dollar volume of payments have declined for both Fedwire and CHIPS. In 1985 overdrafts on Fedwire were 11 percent of total payments. From the third quarter of 1987 through the second quarter of 1988, overdrafts were 9.2 percent of payments. The improvement on CHIPS has been even greater. The net debit positions incurred as a percentage of payments have declined from 15.4 percent to 7.4 percent over

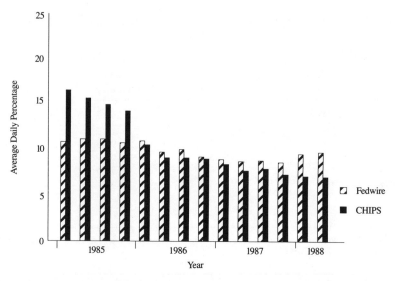

Figure 7-4.   Overdrafts as Share of Payments

the same time period (see Figure 7-4, based on data from the Division of Research and Statistics of the Federal Reserve System, September 1988).

It is possible that the risk reduction policies have slowed the growth rate of risk exposure. Although the original goal of reducing overall risk may not have been achieved, the level of exposure is probably less than it would have been without the caps. One reason for the reduction in overdrafts relative to payments may be that the imposition of caps, even if nonbinding, has focused attention on the problem. The ratio of overdrafts to payments, however, is not a measure of risk exposure.

A better way to measure risk exposure would be to compare the dollar amounts of overdrafts with the ability of other participants to absorb losses in the event of a settlement failure. That comparison would indicate whether the imposition of caps has reduced risk. For the Fed, the terms of the comparison would be the size of the daylight overdraft and the Fed's ability to cover the loss out of either its revenues or its capital account. The risk exposure for a CHIPS participant would be the transfers received during the day to which it has granted its customers immediate access relative to its capital. Unfortunately, those data are not reported.

An alternative method of testing whether the imposition of caps has reduced risk would be to replicate the simulations of settlement failure conducted by Humphrey (1986) using data from after the imposition of caps. His simulation takes into account the capital position of the remaining participants. No more straightforward measure of systemic risk could be devised.

## Moral Hazard and Payment System Risk

The current payment system operates with a substantial amount of risk. Overdraft levels are high and rising. Current caps are not effectively controlling risk. That state of affairs raises the issue of who is bearing the risk. In the event of a settlement failure, where would the losses fall? The answer to that question depends on which transfer system has the failure and how the Federal Reserve responds to the failure.

Consider first a settlement failure occurring on Fedwire. One possibility would be for the Fed to absorb the loss directly. The Fed would initially lose an amount of money equal to the institution's overdraft position. The institution would then be declared insolvent and the Federal Deposit Insurance Corporation or another federal deposit insurance agency would have to deal with the failure. The Fed would be treated like any other unsecured creditor. Given the loss, the Fed's income would be reduced. Because the Fed returns the vast majority of its net income to the U.S. Treasury, any reduction of the Fed's income would probably reduce its payment to the Treasury and thus reduce government receipts.[15] That implies that the taxpaying public would have to make up the shortfall in Treasury receipts, either through new taxes or by repaying additional bonds floated by the government. In the end, the public would indirectly bear the cost.[16]

A second scenario for a settlement failure on Fedwire begins with the Federal Reserve's extending a discount window loan to an institution that is unable to make settlement. Since discount window credit is secured, the status of the Fed would change from that of an unsecured to that of a secured creditor of the troubled institution. The discount window loan could be used for settlement. After settlement, the Fed could call its note and the institution could be declared insolvent. The FDIC or other federal deposit insurer would then have to deal with the failed institution. Typically in such cases, the FDIC wants to find a buyer for the failed institution. The FDIC pays off the Federal Reserve's note in order to gain control of the collateral so that it has clear ownership of the assets to be sold. In that scenario, the Fed would not sustain a loss. Even if the FDIC did not pay off the Fed's note, the Fed would control assets that could be sold to repay the note.

The loss in the second scenario is borne primarily by the FDIC. That situation can be viewed in two ways. One view is that the loss would be small enough for the insurer to absorb out of the insurance fund, and the fund would be replenished by insurance premiums paid by banks. If the loss were too large to be absorbed by the insurer alone, the insurer might require additional congressional funds. If that were the case, the loss would be borne by the taxpaying public.[17]

If a settlement failure were to occur on CHIPS, the Fed's exposure to loss would be largely dependent on whether it acted as a lender of last resort to the failing CHIPS participant, or to other CHIPS participants facing some difficulty in settling, or whether the CHIPS settlement failure caused settlement failure on Fedwire. If the Fed extended a discount window loan to the institution failing to make settlement, then, as described above, the loss would probably fall on the FDIC initially and possibly on the taxpaying public later. Lending to the failing institution would avoid a settlement failure and the systemic risk inherent in such a failure.

If the Fed did not provide a discount window loan to the failing institution, CHIPS would suffer a settlement failure. Previous simulations suggest that a number of additional institutions would be unable to settle. A number of banks might close, and the losses would be borne by bank stockholders, unsecured creditors, other CHIPS participants, the FDIC, and in all likelihood, the taxpaying public. Furthermore, all of the institutions that were unable to settle on CHIPS and were in an overdraft position on Fedwire would be unable to settle their Fedwire accounts. The Fed would probably be exposed to losses equal to the sum of the overdraft positions of the failed institutions. Those Fed losses would be indirectly absorbed by the taxpaying public.

It is unclear whether the loss-sharing arrangement proposed by CHIPS increases or decreases the exposure of the deposit insurance fund. The collateral posted by the failed participant will be used to meet that participant's settlement obligation before any additional settlement obligation is assessed on other participants. Consequently, the loss-sharing agreement gives CHIPS participants first claim on the collateral. Therefore, if the failed participant is an insured depository institution, the deposit insurance fund will take into possession fewer assets than it would have without the loss-sharing agreement. That simple view ignores the substantial costs that might result from a settlement failure that resulted in a systemic failure of other CHIPS participants. As a result, it is impossible to know whether the deposit insurance fund is made better or worse off by the loss-sharing agreement (Mengle 1990).

The scenarios make it clear that the taxpaying public is indirectly bearing a large part of the payment system risk. The Fed can either bear a loss or shift the cost to the FDIC, other federal deposit insurers, or other participants in the payment system. If the Fed bears the initial loss, the result will be lower government receipts at the U.S. Treasury. If the FDIC or another insurer bears the loss, it is very possible that congressional funding will be needed to replenish the deposit insurance funds. In either case, directly or indirectly, the taxpaying public may incur the loss.

The major problem with a system in which the public bears the risk is that the public has little or no control over the level of risk. Usually, a free market assigns risk to those best able to control it, or if that is not possible, risk is assigned to those who are best able either to diversify the risk or to absorb the loss. The taxpaying public may be able only to absorb resulting losses. A moral hazard exists because the participants in the payment systems have relatively little incentive to control their risk exposure, especially on Fedwire. The public is dependent on the Federal Reserve to act as its agent to control risk.

Participants in the payment systems do not do enough to control their risk. There are two explanations for their excessive risk taking. The first has to do with the externalities created by the extension of intraday credit. The second explanation revolves around expectations about how the Fed will respond to settlement failures on either Fedwire or CHIPS.

When a bank increases the amount of intraday credit it extends to another participant in the payment system, it shares the increased risk of failure of the second institution with all other participants that have extended intraday credit to the same borrower. Furthermore, by extending credit, the first bank increases the risk to its own creditors. Such increases in risk represent costs that are not priced in the extension of intraday credit.[18] Those externalities, however, apply to all extensions of credit whether they are intraday, overnight, or term loans. In most interday extensions of credit, the lender restricts the amount of additional credit the borrower can obtain. Those restrictions are typically referred to as loan covenants, and the violation of a loan covenant permits the lender to either renegotiate or withdraw the loan.

In the case of increased risk incurred by a payment system participant that extends additional credit, the creditors could also act to control the risk taking of the participant. A simple approach would be for a bank to set a bilateral net credit limit for other participants and to establish covenants the violation of which would change the bilateral limit. The covenants might be a limit on the total net debit position of the intraday borrower. The present rules on CHIPS may reflect an attempt to deal with that externality.

Second, participants in the wire transfer system do not control their risk exposure because they expect that the Fed, by lending through the discount window, will prevent any settlement failure and, consequently, any systemic failures. Since payment system participants expect the Fed to absorb the risk, they do not factor it into their willingness to extend intraday credit. Thus, creditor institutions often abdicate their duty to monitor risk and rely on the Fed, other regulatory agencies, or the deposit insurers to control the risk-taking behavior of payment system participants. That kind of behavior is analogous to uninsured depositors of large banks expecting the federal deposit insurer to handle any failure with a purchase-and-assumption transaction that will leave them whole. Consequently, those depositors are not motivated to control their exposure to risk.

As the result of either externalities or expectations of a government bailout, participants do too little to control their exposure to risk because the marginal cost to society of an additional dollar of intraday credit is much higher than the expected marginal cost to the participant that extends the credit. In addition, institutions that regularly build large daylight overdrafts treat the marginal cost of additional intraday credit as near zero when their overdraft cap is not binding. Even the cost of exceeding a cap may be too low if the penalty is being "counseled" by the Fed.

## Reforming the Payment System

The key to reducing payment system risk is to restructure the current system in a way that shifts the costs of the risks to the participants that are best able to reduce the level of risk. The Fed is currently exploring policies that would raise the marginal cost of risk to the participant to a level closer to the marginal social cost of the actual risk. The Fed is committed to imposing a fee on institutions that use intraday credit, and it has discussed the theoretically optimal level of such credit. Charging for daylight overdrafts could reduce risk taking substantially because it would encourage the adoption of several readily implemented institutional changes that would lower risks. For example, the maturities on federal funds loans could be extended from overnight to several days, continuing contracts or rollover contracts on federal funds could be instituted, and netting by novation could be introduced.[19] The Fed has estimated that if those institutional changes were adopted, daylight overdrafts could be nearly eliminated.

Pricing daylight overdrafts is intuitively appealing, especially to economists who believe that once an appropriate price is set, agents will behave in an optimal manner. But the Fed's price for daylight overdrafts will be unlikely to achieve an ideal solution in the case of payment system risk. There is an implicit assumption that the Fed will be able to set a price equal to the marginal social cost of overdrafts. Any difference between those two costs will result in a level of daylight overdrafts that is either too high or too low.

Several suggestions for pricing intraday credit have been made. One is to price daylight overdrafts at the same price as intraday credit extended by banks to securities dealers. An alternative suggestion is to price daylight overdrafts at the same rate as federal funds advances adjusted for the duration of the overdraft position. While the latter would be more technically difficult, it would reduce both the size and the duration of overdrafts. One key advantage of both pricing schemes is that they attempt to tie the price of daylight overdrafts to a price determined in the marketplace. Both pricing schemes, however, have their flaws.[20]

Setting the correct price for daylight overdrafts would be nearly impossible for the Federal Reserve. The suggested pricing schemes are reasonable first attempts to set an average price that might be relatively close to correct, but they offer no way of determining the risk premium that ought to be assigned to each individual institution. Furthermore, it is possible that the price charged for intraday credit to securities dealers, and to a lesser extent the interest rate on federal funds, is affected by the current structure of the payment system. Determining the appropriate price for daylight overdrafts is an extremely complex problem for a government entity. Numerous examples of pricing errors in centrally planned economies can be cited. Such errors regularly create either gluts or shortages of goods that are far less complex in nature and theoretically easier to price than are daylight overdrafts.

Even if an appropriate price could be determined, would it be charged? The Fed has a history of not charging a market-clearing price for the extension of credit, not responding to changes in the price of credit determined in the marketplace, and preferring to ration credit by means other than price. Discount window lending is the interday equivalent of intraday credit extensions. The federal funds market offers an excellent reference by which discount window credits could be priced. As shown in Figure 7–5 (based on data from various issues of the *Federal Reserve Bulletin*), the divergence of the federal funds and discount rates is at times substantial and rarely constant. Because the discount rate is typically below the federal funds rate, extensions of credit through the discount window are rationed by nonprice means. Is there any reason to believe that the Fed

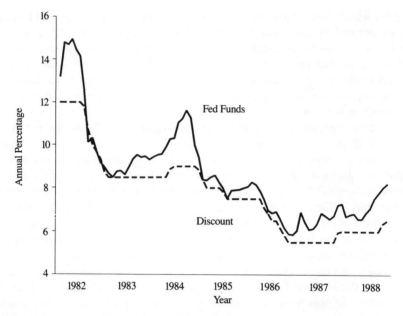

Figure 7–5.   Short-Term Interest Rates

would do a better job of pricing intraday credit than it currently does of pricing interday credit?

An alternative solution would be to eliminate extensions of intraday credit over Fedwire. As easily as the Fed permits overdrafts, it could eliminate them by mandate. Though some technical difficulties exist, the Fed could establish a system of real-time monitoring for all participating institutions and refuse any transaction that would create an overdraft. The CHIPS system already has that capability. That approach would create a market for intraday federal funds, and the public would be relieved of the risk of loss that could result from a settlement failure. Banks extending credit through the intraday federal funds market would have as much incentive to monitor their risk as they currently do in the overnight federal funds market.[21]

Eliminating daylight overdrafts on Fedwire would affect monetary policy. There would be a tremendous increase in the demand for reserves. Thus, it might be necessary to move to a system with zero daylight overdrafts by gradually lowering the caps. Such a managed shock to the demand for reserves would be far more predictable than the shock to the financial system caused by a settlement failure, especially one that resulted in systemic failures.

## Summary and Conclusion

Risk within the payment system is perceived as a serious problem; however, there is a lack of hard empirical evidence by which to measure actual risk exposure. There has never been a settlement failure. Although large banks have failed, none of those failures has been so completely unexpected as to have occurred in a single day and thus prevented regulators from controlling their risk taking in the payment system. Currently, overdrafts are measured either absolutely or relative to the volume of payments. It would, however, be better to measure overdrafts relative to the capital available to absorb the risk. Finally, the likelihood of systemic failure as the result of a settlement failure has not been measured since the imposition of bilateral credit caps, net debit caps, and cross-system caps.

The imposition of caps appears to have had some effect, but the caps are not solving the problem. Currently, caps are too high to be binding on the majority of participants in the payment systems. Since caps were imposed, overdrafts have grown at a slower rate than have total transactions, which suggests that caps are having some effect, but total overdrafts have continued to rise.

The current structure places a great deal of any risk in the payment system on the general public. In the event of a settlement or systemic failure, the loss will be at least partially borne by either the Federal Reserve or the FDIC. A large loss will either affect the Treasury's receipts in the case of the Federal Reserve or require an expenditure of funds in the case of the FDIC. Consequently, taxpayers, who have limited ability to control risk in the payment system, are bearing at least part of that risk. The exposure of the public indicates that there is a negative externality in the extension of intraday credit.

The most direct way to compensate for that externality is to price it. Currently, intraday extensions of credit are not priced. The Federal Reserve is committed to pricing daylight overdrafts in order to encourage their reduction, but history has shown that the Fed is not likely to price overdrafts at a rate that eliminates the public's exposure.

The Federal Reserve could pursue an alternative approach. First, the Fed could gradually lower the current caps to zero, effectively no longer permitting daylight overdrafts. That approach would require a substantial injection of reserves and would encourage the development of an intraday federal funds market.[22] It would require the Fed to improve its current computer system to provide real-time accounting for all participants. It would shift the risk back to the banking institutions. Those institutions would then have the proper incentives to control their risks.[23] Finally, it would encourage the development of a private market for intraday credit instead of government pricing of such credit.

## Notes

1. See, for example, Association of Reserve City Bankers (1984), Task Force on Controlling Payment System Risk (1988b), Humphrey (1986), and Mengle (1985).

2. Banks also transfer funds for their own purposes, often to other banks. In those transfers the sender and the sending bank are one and the same as are the receiver and the receiving bank.

3. Fedwire can be accessed by banks, savings-and-loan associations, and credit unions. To simplify the exposition, all participants will be referred to as banks.

4. "Optimal" in this case means the amount of intraday credit for which the marginal social benefit of the last dollar of intraday credit exactly equals its marginal social cost. See Task Force on Controlling Payment System Risk (August 1988a, pp. 26–27).

5. Settlement risk is also referred to as credit risk by some authors.

6. It is possible that the loss would be less if liquidation of the failed institution provided funds for a partial payment or if the FDIC, as guarantor of the failed institution's liabilities, reimbursed the Fed.

7. Systemic risk is not possible on Fedwire because the Federal Reserve bears any loss.

8. If the failure occurred on the CHIPS system, there would be a real possibility of multiple failures resulting from the unwind.

9. Failure to settle for technical reasons is not discussed, though it has nearly occurred. Usually such problems result from computer failures, and in the past they have been dealt with by extending credit through the discount window to permit the affected institution to settle.

10. The Federal Reserve System does not specify how the net debit cap should be set. CHIPS sets its net debit cap as 5 to 6 percent of the sum of all bilateral net credit caps granted to a participant by other participants. See New York Clearing House Association (1988).

11. An institution's net credit position on CHIPS would not increase its net debit cap on the Fedwire system to more than the cross-system cap.

12. Initially, the institutions that were monitored on a real-time basis on Fedwire were financially troubled institutions and the U.S. branches and agencies of foreign banks. The former were included because they are judged to run a high risk of failure and the latter because the Federal Reserve may find it difficult to monitor the behavior of the parent company. The Federal Reserve is expanding its ability to monitor institutions on a real-time basis, and it is now monitoring the largest users of Fedwire services regardless of their financial condition.

13. The concern about overdrafts resulting from book-entry securities transfers may be misplaced because the securities themselves can serve as collateral for the transaction. That issue has not yet been fully resolved.

14. The October 1985 date should have affected only the CHIPS system. Any effect

on the Fedwire system would probably have been to increase the level of overdrafts. Once CHIPS implemented a cap, institutions that reached their cap could avoid the CHIPS limitation by sending transfers on the Fedwire system. There is some limit to that practice, however, because Fedwire imposed similar caps only five months after CHIPS did.

15. In 1987 the Federal Reserve made a payment to the Treasury of $17.7 billion. Board of Governors of the Federal Reserve System (1988, p. 201).

16. An alternative approach would be for the Federal Reserve to treat the loss as a cost of providing wire transfer services. In that case the Fed would need to recoup the loss through higher prices on future wire transfers. The Fed, however, has never attempted to price its wire transfer services so as to recover any of the cost of risk exposure. Furthermore, to recoup a $1 billion loss in the year that it occurred would require raising the basic price of a Fedwire transfer from $0.50 to $18.68. Pricing after the fact would be ineffective since the Fed would simply lose business to competing wire transfer systems.

17. Any doubt that a congressional bailout would occur has been eliminated by the Bush administration's rescue of the savings-and-loan industry's insurance fund.

18. For a complete discussion, see Task Force on Controlling Payment System Risk (1988a, p. 27).

19. Netting by novation is a technique whereby gross bilateral transfers between two institutions are replaced by a new contractual obligation to transfer only the net amount.

20. It has been suggested that even a price that does not exactly equate marginal social costs with marginal private costs would still be helpful in reducing payment system risk. I would not argue against that suggestion as a second-best solution. Any price for daylight overdrafts would reflect at least some of the cost of risk exposure and would probably reduce payment system risk.

21. It might be argued that the existence of the safety nets of deposit insurance and discount window loans reduces the incentive to monitor risk. While that is probably the case, it is a problem that lies outside the scope of this paper.

22. Any arguments that the shock of injecting reserves would make the control of monetary policy more difficult would be countered by the argument that a systemic failure in the payment system is likely to produce a much larger and much less manageable shock.

23. One possible hindrance to that solution is the moral hazard created by the existence of the federal safety nets of deposit insurance and discount window loans. Insuring deposits may eliminate or reduce risk premiums on deposits and encourage depository institutions to take excessive risks.

## References

Association of Reserve City Bankers. 1984. *The Final Report of the Risk Control Task Force*. Washington, D.C.: ARCB.

Belton, Terrence M., Gelfand, Matthew D., Humphrey, David B., and Marquardt, Jeffrey C. 1987. "Daylight Overdrafts and Payments System Risk," *Federal Reserve Bulletin* 73 (November): 839–52.

Board of Governors of the Federal Reserve System. 1988. *74th Annual Report, 1987*. Washington D.C.: Board of Governors.

Clair, Robert T. Forthcoming. "The Clearing House Interbank Payment System." *Research in Financial Services: Private and Public* 3.

Federal Reserve Bank of New York. 1987–88. "Large-Dollar Payment Flows from New York." *Quarterly Review* 12 (Winter): 6–13.

Humphrey, David Burras. 1984. *The U.S. Payments System: Costs, Pricing, Competition and Risk*. Monograph Series in Finance and Economics. New York: Salomon Brothers Center for the Study of Financial Institutions, Graduate School of Business Administration, New York University.

Humphrey, David Burras. 1986. "Payments Finality and Risk of Settlement Failure." In *Technology and the Regulation of Financial Markets: Securities, Futures, and Banking*, edited by Anthony Saunders and Lawrence J. White, pp. 97–120. Lexington, Mass.: Lexington Books.

Mengle, David L. 1985. "Daylight Overdrafts and Payments System Risks." Federal Reserve Bank of Richmond *Economic Review* 71 (May/June): 14–27.

Mengle, David L. 1990. "Legal and Regulatory Reform in Electronic Payments: An Evaluation of Payment Finality Rules." In *The U.S. Payment System: Efficiency, Risk, and the Role of the Federal Reserve*, proceedings of a symposium on the U.S. payment system sponsored by the Federal Reserve Bank of Richmond, May 25–26, 1988, edited by David B. Humphrey, pp. 145–80. Boston: Kluwer Academic Publishers.

New York Clearing House Association. 1988. *Constitution of the New York Clearing House Association with Rules and Regulations*. New York: NYCHA.

Task Force on Controlling Payment System Risk. 1988a. *Controlling Risk in the Payments System*. Washington, D.C.: Board of Governors, August.

Task Force on Controlling Payment System Risk. 1988b. *A Strategic Plan for Managing Risk in the Payments System*. Washington, D.C.: Board of Governors, August.

# 8 PAYMENT SYSTEM RISK: A PRIVATE-SECTOR VIEW

## Gerard F. Milano

It is useful to begin a discussion of payment system risk with a brief over-view of the payment system itself so that we can share a common under-standing of the mechanism, its size, and its complexity before we begin to discuss the questions of risk. I shall present some basic statistics on the overall size of the payment system, discuss some of the mechanics, and then examine the question of the so-called daylight overdraft and describe how the Federal Reserve views that phenomenon. Finally, I will try to describe some of the proposed remedies for daylight overdrafts and some other remedies that are not so freely discussed.

Table 8–1 is based on a recent Federal Reserve Board "Electronic Clearing House Study" for Congress (1988a). Various kinds of payments and transaction volumes are listed in the appendices of that study. Since this is a discussion of intraday credit risk in payments, usually referred to by the Fed's pet term "daylight overdrafts," I put the volumes on a daily

---

The author is executive director of the California Bankers Clearing House Association. The opinions expressed are those of the author and do not necessarily reflect the views of the California Bankers Clearing House Association or any of its members.

Table 8-1.   Daily Average Volumes and Values for the U.S. Payment Systems

| Type of Transaction | Daily Average Volume (Thousands) | Daily Average Value ($ Millions) |
|---|---|---|
| Checks | 179,283 | 119,522 |
| ACH | 2,789 | 1,859 |
| ATM | 17,131 | 857 |
| Bank cards | 4,781 | 622 |
| Subtotal | 203,984 | 122,860 |
| CHIPS | 114 | 608,000 |
| Fedwire funds | 212 | 605,000 |
| Fedwire securities | 8 | 358,000 |
| Total | 204,318 | 1,683,860 |

*Note:* ACH = automated clearinghouse, ATM = automatic teller machine, CHIPS = Clearing House Interbank Payment System.

average basis and added estimates of value. Various sources, including Clair (1991), were used for the estimates.

Values approaching $1.7 trillion a day raise questions about how that much money is spent or invested and who is transferring the funds. I was unable to find any research on that topic, so I developed some rough estimates using the domestic financial statistics given in the August 1988 issue of the *Federal Reserve Bulletin* (Federal Reserve Board 1988b) as my primary source. The most consistent run of data in the August issue is for the quarter ending March 1988.

My results are presented in Table 8-2. The first grouping includes transactions involving overnight funds, repos,[1] and other short-term borrowing. The overnight transactions are estimated at 75 percent of the total value outstanding on March 30.[2] The 75 percent estimate is multiplied by two because in overnight funds markets the borrower repays the overnight loan early in the day, and the lender, having secured his repayment and shopped the funds markets, recommits the funds to the same or another borrower later in the day. Hence the same value is transferred twice each day. The $383 billion figure is based on the assumption that the market is approximated by large borrowing banks (A 19).[3]

I based my estimate for government securities transactions on Clair (1991), who indicates a daily transaction value that is roughly four times the daily average value of net securities sales published in the Fed's government securities dealer series (A 31). The difference is explained by

Table 8-2.   Estimated Value of U.S. Payments, March 1988

| Source[a] | Type of Transaction | factor | Daily Value of Transactions ($ Millions) |
|---|---|---|---|
| *Financial Markets* | | | |
| A 19 | Overnight funds transactions | 75% of value × 2 | 382,775 |
| A 31 | U.S. Treasury securities | 4 times value | 362,560 |
| A 23 | Commercial paper | 4 times value | 68,052 |
| A 25 | New York Stock Exchange | 75% of value | 20,439 |
| A 25 | American Stock Exchange | 75% of value | 2,759 |
| WSJ | Commodities futures, options, etc. | At value | 37,301 |
| | Subtotal | | 873,886 |
| *Domestic Commercial Payments* | | | |
| A 51 | Wages and salaries (nongovernment) | | 7,451 |
| A 51 | Services | | 6,557 |
| A 51 | Nondurable goods | × 10 | 39,780 |
| A 51 | U.S. government receipts | | 2,858 |
| A 51 | Nonresidential structures & equipment | × 10 | 19,040 |
| A 51 | Durable goods | × 10 | 16,890 |
| A 51 | Interest | × 10 | 14,240 |
| A 51 | Residential structures | × 10 | 9,050 |
| A 51 | Inventories | × 10 | 2,300 |
| | Subtotal | | 118,166 |
| *International Trade Payments* | | | |
| A 51 | Exports | × 10 | 19,350 |
| A 51 | Imports | × 10 | 23,780 |
| | Subtotal | | 43,130 |
| | Total value of daily payments | | 1,035,182 |

[a] Information from the *Wall Street Journal* (WSJ) and the following charts published by the Federal Reserve Board (1988b):
A 19 Assets and liabilities of large commercial banks
A 23 Commercial paper and bankers' dollar acceptances
A 25 Stock market—selected statistics
A 31 U.S. government securities dealers' transactions
A 51 Gross national product and income

the fact that the Fed reports net securities sales, but Clair indicates that there may be as many as three layers of intervening dealers between the ultimate buyers and sellers in the securities market. Thus, total transactions represent a multiple of the value of the securities actually transferred. The commercial paper market (A 23) accounts for another $17 billion a day. I assume that the commercial paper market has the same kind of structure as the government securities market, and I therefore multiplied the daily average value from the Fed *Bulletin* by four to produce the estimate shown.

The stock market figures required some estimates too. To start, I simply took the daily average transactions for the two large exchanges and multiplied by the average value of shares traded on each exchange. The New York and American Stock exchanges combined averaged almost 190 million shares a day and had average share values of approximately $150 and $300, respectively, accounting for about $31 billion a day in combined volume on the two exchanges. I estimated that 25 percent of the trades each day would be completed in house and would not require a settled trade between brokers. Thus, the numbers in Table 8–2 represent 75 percent of the average shares traded on each exchange multiplied by the average price per share. Finally, I took the average values for commodities futures and options listed in the *Wall Street Journal*, multiplied them by the trading volumes, and came up with a crude estimate of daily value of $37 billion. Those calculations produce a daily value of some $874 billion for financial market transactions.

For the Domestic and International sections of Table 8–2, I used the gross national product and the national income series to estimate the March 31, 1988, values at the daily average transaction rate for the first quarter of 1988. Recognizing that the goods and services measured by GNP require a host of individual transactions among manufacturers, dealers, and consumers, I multiplied the values in the GNP series by 10 to more closely approximate the daily transaction values they represent.[4] Wages, services, and government receipts are shown at the daily average rate without a multiplier on the assumption that those transactions are largely handled directly between suppliers and consumers. Summing each category yields $118 billion in daily domestic commercial payments and $43 billion in international trade payments. U.S. government transactions are excluded on the assumption that they are riskless.

As is readily apparent, that approach left me more than $648 billion short of the more traditional measures of average daily transaction values reported in Table 8–1. Government transactions came to mind, but government transactions are excluded from the volume statistics in Table 8–1. It did not seem reasonable to increase the GNP multipliers to make up the slack, but it did occur to me that the difference might be reasonably attributed to locational transfers (usually called cash concentration or cash management).[5] Given the choices of more than 10 layers of middleman transactions, grossly overstated estimates of payment volumes, grossly

Table 8–3.  Summary of Estimates

| Transaction Group | Daily Average Dollar Value ($ Millions) | Percentage of Value |
|---|---|---|
| Financial markets | 873,886 | 51.9 |
| Domestic commercial | 118,166 | 7.0 |
| International trade | 43,130 | 2.6 |
| Transfers (residual) | 648,738 | 38.5 |
| Total payments | 1,683,920 | 100.0 |

understated GNP, or the very popular use of cash management by corporations and financial intermediaries, I opted for cash management. It seems reasonable to me that financial market activity of almost $900 billion a day would require a fairly healthy volume of cash concentration. I thus attributed the residual $648.7 billion to cash management transfers.

To summarize, by my estimates just over 50 percent of the volume of daily payments serve the financial markets, just under 10 percent are for goods and services bought and sold in domestic and foreign markets, and about 40 percent involve deposit transfers in which the same owner moves money from one institution to another (see Table 8–3).

## Payment Mechanisms

It is generally accepted that the original clearinghouses were coffee shops or other drinking places. Bank messengers found it more convenient, more pleasant, and perhaps safer to assemble in a coffee shop and swap their packages than to travel from bank to bank to make their deliveries.[6] When bank management became involved in the private clearinghouses that evolved from the coffee shop rendezvous, they developed net clearing procedures to reduce the total value of transfers necessary to settle the daily exchange of items. The netting process itself was viewed as a safety measure because settlements were originally completed in gold. Transporting bullion clearly represented significant risk. Netting the transactions between participants kept the values of hard currency in transit to a minimum and helped conserve specie during liquidity crises. Later the bullion was immobilized in vaults and vault receipts backed by gold became the medium for settlement.

During the financial crisis of 1907, many local clearinghouses placed discounted loan documents and Treasury bonds in their vaults. The clearinghouse members circulated the vault receipts as scrip. Congress institutionalized those practices in 1913 by creating the Federal Reserve System, which has turned the circulation of bank notes backed by Treasury securities into its most profitable activity.[7]

Today the amount of money that is handled by clearinghouses, including those run by the regional Federal Reserve Banks, is substantial. For example, check clearing in the 25 largest U.S. cities, excluding New York, reached an average of $12.103 billion a day during the week ended March 30, 1988. New York cleared an average of $21.797 billion a day in checks and $608.743 billion on CHIPS.[8]

But what happens in a net settlement system if one or more banks that owe money to the other institutions cannot meet their obligations? In a traditional bankers' clearinghouse, the members demand the return of the checks they presented to the illiquid bank and charge those returns back to their own depositors. That puts the credit risk associated with settlement squarely in the hands of the original holder or payee of the check. Private wire systems like CHIPS evolved from that basic approach to netting and established an "unwinding" procedure based on the check-clearing system to reverse the items in the event of an end-of-day liquidity problem.

The Fed uses the same netting method to settle the transactions among its 12 district banks every day. However, some years ago the Fed came to the conclusion that an unwinding procedure was unworkable for the 12 district reserve banks and their thousands of local customers.

Indeed, it would be a complex task to unravel a day's transactions among all the financial institutions that deal with any one of the 12 district banks. The problem is further compounded by interdistrict wire transfers among the 12 reserve banks. Returning all the checks presented locally to one failed bank is a fairly straightforward process. Returning wire transfers nationwide is quite another thing. In fact, wire transfers represent a major complication of the simple clearinghouse system just described.

Checks are a debit transfer system. The check (or debit) is a promise to pay on presentment. In the simplest check transaction, the collector gives a credit to the depositor's account and presents the debit for payment to the bank on which it is drawn. If the check is not good, the payor bank returns the check, and the collecting bank sends it back to the payee and reverses the original deposit credit. If the collecting bank extends credit by letting its depositor draw funds before it has completed presentment, the bank stands to lose if the customer does not replace the funds.

Wire transfers represent a credit transfer. Credit transfer systems are more efficient than debit transfers because the costly, time-consuming step of presentment is eliminated. With a wire transfer, the payor initiates the transfer by issuing a promise to pay at settlement. The receiver of the wire then creates a credit in the customer's account. Incoming and outgoing wires are totaled automatically for each participating bank as they are sent and received. At the end of the day the totals are netted and settled.

The return process, which serves as a safety valve in debit transfers, is eliminated for wire transfers. If there is a problem with a transaction, the sending bank contacts the receiver and asks the receiving bank to initiate another wire to reverse the transaction. Because there is no presentment or return process, wire systems rely heavily on the sending bank's promise to pay at settlement. If the sending bank cannot make good on its promise at settlement time, the credit transfer system is faced with a dilemma. It can create a credit pool through which other member institutions advance the necessary funds to the illiquid institution, or it can attempt to reverse some or all of the transactions until it reaches a settlement value that can be sustained. The latter process is called an "unwind." Until a solution to the dilemma can be found and a settlement achieved, the receiving banks will sustain losses unless they recover funds credited to their depositors before settlement.

In private credit transfer systems like CHIPS, the sending bank's promise to pay is bolstered with credit limits. Each institution can limit the value of wires it will accept from any other participant. The limits can be adjusted during the day so that new information can be quickly factored into each bank's controls. The credit limits give CHIPS wire transfer system participants protection from unwanted credit risk by preventing receipt of wires above a limit set by the receiver and thereby providing a safety valve for prudent institutions. Credit limits also provide a cushion for the system operator. It can attempt to arrange a pool of credit for an illiquid institution at settlement on the presumption that no participant extended more credit than it was willing to risk. If the pool fails to come together, the operator can require an unwind, which leaves individual banks to their own devices for recovering credits from depositors.

In a national system like Fedwire with its thousands of senders and receivers, the cost of maintaining lines of credit from one bank to another would represent a very large operating burden on the system. Returning wires would be a difficult task compounded further by the nationwide scope of the system. Thus, the Fed's policy of "instant finality" for Fedwire has evolved. Instead of unwinding the day's payment messages or canceling the credits sent by the illiquid bank, the Fed puts its own credit on the line to cover the debit side of a Fedwire transaction, which protects the receiving institutions, the credit side, from a settlement loss. A receiving bank is not required to limit the credit risk it will accept from initiating institutions; it can rely on the Fed's credit instead. Thus, the Fed has "solved" the problem of unscrambling all the wires from an illiquid institution by replacing an operating problem, how to unravel the transactions, with credit risk. Instead of spreading the risk to all recipients, each of whom protects itself, as CHIPS does, the Fed takes the risk on itself to avoid the operational problem of unraveling the transactions. The Fed's policy reflects its determination that a certain amount of credit risk is preferable to a continuing operating cost for maintaining receiver credit limits for thousands of financial institutions. How large is the credit risk created by the Fed's policy? That question brings us to the issue of daylight overdrafts.

## Daylight Overdrafts

What are "daylight overdrafts"? How do they occur? Why are they a problem, and for whom? What measures are being taken to avoid or reduce them? Do those measures work? What other measures are possible?

When the Fed first started worrying about the exposure inherent in its guarantee of Fedwire payments, it instructed its staff to estimate total credit exposure. The staff studied Fedwire transactions hour by hour throughout the day and discovered that payments do not flow in orderly sequences between initiators of wires and receivers. Some institutions receive funds early in the day but do not send funds out until later.[9] By examining the transactions in order of occurrence, the Fed discovered that negative balances would appear in some reserve accounts if the transactions were posted as they occurred during the day. But by the time the entire day's transactions were netted at the close of business, those negative balances had disappeared. The Federal Reserve staff called that phenomenon a daylight overdraft. Daylight overdrafts are used as a measure of the Fed's *potential* exposure to an end-of-day settlement failure. That potential exposure might have remained just an interesting phenomenon for the Federal Reserve staff to study, but the Federal Reserve Board of Governors determined that it was not enough to monitor the Fed's own credit risk; they decided to supervise the intraday credit practices of private clearinghouses as well.

According to the Fed, a daylight overdraft occurs when a depository institution either transfers more money than it has on deposit in its reserve account or transfers more money over a private network than it has already received. Although it is clear that the Fed might have a collection problem with an illiquid institution because Fedwire had guaranteed the bank's payments, it is less apparent why the Fed should include payments made on a private transfer system like CHIPS in its definition of daylight overdrafts.

The Fed defends its supervision of intraday credit on private networks as follows: If a participant in a private system (like CHIPS) were unable to cover its settlement obligation at the end of the day, that bank would apply to the Fed for a loan. The Fed would then be in the position of risking damage to the other participants in the private wire system if it refused the loan. In addition, innocent beneficiaries of the wires could be asked to return credits originated by the illiquid bank. That line of reasoning has led the Fed to use a measurement system designed by its staff to monitor the credit risk exposure created by its Fedwire guarantee policy to also monitor intraday credit policies of private wire networks that create potential demand for discount window services. It should be noted that the Fed does not guarantee CHIPS payments, nor has CHIPS asked for a Fed guarantee. CHIPS uses Fedwire only to send final end-of-day net settlement payments.

Both the private clearing systems and the Federal Reserve use reserve account balances at the regional Federal Reserve Banks to settle their transactions. Reserve balances at the Fed amounted to approximately $35.7 billion at the end of March 1988, and average daily transactions were approximately $1.7 trillion (Table 8–1). The ratio between daily payments and the reserve balances used to settle them is almost 50 to 1: the ratio of Fedwires to reserve balances is 27 to 1, and the ratio of daily payments to reserve balances is 47 to 1. The high ratio of daily transactions to daily average reserve balances is certainly one important explanation of daylight overdrafts, but three other factors are also cited as causes of daylight overdrafts. The speed of the mechanism used by Fedwire for debiting and crediting reserve accounts determines the number of transfers that can be accommodated while maintaining positive reserve balances. The flow of payments between institutions and their customers determines the relative balance in each reserve account at any given moment. Finally, the fact that there is no explicit charge for the Fedwire guarantee or for intraday credit encourages depository institutions to run larger overdrafts than they might otherwise.

Daylight overdrafts at the Fed can be reduced by taking one or more of the following actions:

1. raising reserve requirements, which would create a higher base to support funds transfer activity;

2.  improving the flow of transfers (e.g., by installing faster, more efficient Fed computers);
3.  restricting the flow itself (slower, more balanced traffic); and
4.  increasing the price of daylight credit.

To date the Fed has avoided requiring increased reserves to reduce daylight overdrafts, presumably because increasing reserves has monetary policy side effects that the Fed does not want to face. As a practical matter, however, the Fed would face a significant political challenge from all depository institutions, including banks, thrifts, and credit unions, if it imposed higher reserve requirements. It is possible that the Fed could require higher reserve balances from a handful of so-called overdrafting institutions. The Fed has, in effect, already raised the ante for major securities dealers by perfecting its collateral interest in the securities underlying its securities transfer service.

Some improvements have been made in the speed with which funds are transferred, but recent Federal Reserve efforts to improve its technology have concentrated on replacing manual access to Fedwire with personal computer hookups for smaller institutions. Such efforts are probably designed more to increase the use of Fedwire by smaller institutions and to reduce the costs of Fedwire operations than to decrease credit risk by increasing payment transfer speed. In fact, as access to Fedwire through personal computer hookups has spread, many smaller banks have shifted their wire transfer payments from their large correspondent banks to their regional Federal Reserve Banks. Such competition by regional reserve banks reduces correspondent balances, which makes larger institutions more dependent on borrowed funds. Increased dependence on borrowed funds of course increases volume in the Fed funds market and creates large reserve deficiencies for correspondent institutions each morning when they repay their overnight loans. Thus, regional reserve bank competition for correspondent services has helped increase daylight overdrafts on Fedwire.

The possibility of reducing daylight overdrafts by increasing the processing capacity of the Fed's computer services has been largely ignored by the Federal Reserve. The lack of capital reinvestment by reserve banks can be attributed to the difficulties of maintaining significant portfolio earnings in a period of stable to declining interest rates and significant federal deficits. The Fed protects its political independence by returning a large portion of its portfolio earnings to the Treasury. Capital expenditures on the Fedwire system would require higher retained earnings and would lower the Fed's transfers to the Treasury. Reduced payments to the Treasury might lead to increased congressional scrutiny and intervention in Federal Reserve affairs. Without a significant increase in the reinvestment of Federal Reserve earnings in Fedwire equipment, however, reductions in daylight overdrafts as a result of more efficient reserve bank processing will not occur any time soon. Viewed another way, daylight overdrafts are caused in part by the Federal Reserve's failure to maintain processing capacity equal to the demand for transfers. Breakdowns in Fedwire computer rooms and telecommunications systems also boost the daylight overdraft level.

If the Fed cannot speed traffic, it might try to slow it. In fact, flow restrictions have been used by the Federal Reserve in the past to curb its credit exposure. Wire traffic restrictions, measured and restrained to date, have been enacted in the form of net debit caps (i.e., limits on the net value of wire payments sent by individual banks). Specific debit caps are set for different institutions on the basis of multiples of each bank's primary capital. The multiples applied have been reduced gradually over time.[10] Thus, instead of taking the steps necessary to increase its processing capacity, the Federal Reserve has, to some extent, shifted the burden of controlling risk to the institutions initiating Fedwires by imposing limits on their ability to generate transfers. Control costs also fall on the regulatory agencies that are more directly involved in banking supervision than is the Federal Reserve.[11]

Given that the Federal Reserve Board of Governors is composed of economists, it is not surprising that the focus of attention at the Fed is shifting away from regulated traffic flows toward pricing daylight credit. In my view the advocates of regulation among the Federal Reserve staff are not ready to give up their regulatory hold, and consequently it will be some time before a market-priced system replaces the regulatory caps now in place. It is more likely that the regulatory bias of the Fed staff will lead the Federal Reserve Board to conclude that pricing alone is insufficient to maintain control. Both pricing and regulation are probable as long as the Fed staff continues to influence Federal Reserve Board decisions on the issue.

It may be useful at this point to quickly review developments in private payment services. By their nature private systems are more efficient than Fedwire. First, they serve a smaller number of participants, creating a more concentrated flow of traffic. Second, private systems do not face the same bureaucratic constraints as Fedwire does when they perceive a need to upgrade their equipment. A faster CHIPS system was already in place when the Fed first required real-time controls. Although the costs of installing controls mandated by the Fed and maintaining real-time monitors have cut into the productive capacity of CHIPS, the credit control innovations implemented by that system have kept pace with traffic growth thus far.[12]

Other private payment networks have not managed as well as CHIPS, however. Since the Federal Reserve Board imposed its credit control requirements, four private electronic networks have turned off their systems. Bankwire, General Electric Information Service's Automated Clearing House, the Chicago Clearing House's Clearing House Electronic Settlement System, and California's Pacific Rim Electronic Settlement Service have all terminated operations. California's Automated Clearing House Association, with operating services provided by VISA, continues to negotiate with the Federal Reserve over an agreement by which Fedwire would provide end-of-day settlement services. The Fed is supposedly required to provide such services under the provisions of the 1980 Depository Institutions Deregulation and Monetary Control Act. Yet the Federal Reserve operations and legal staff has been unable to design an effective settlement agreement with Fedwire's private competitors despite efforts over eight years. That logjam has stymied new payment services' experimenting with other technologies or alternate arrangements. Such new services, it should be noted, might produce other answers to the credit risk question.

What about new ideas from CHIPS? Given that Corrigan (1987), the president of the Federal Reserve Bank of New York, publicly concluded that the problem of payment system risk could be resolved if CHIPS would only turn over management control to the Fed, we might expect the New York Clearing House to counter with other alternatives. Although CHIPS has offered no detailed public rebuttal of Corrigan, it would not be surprising if CHIPS were to consider requiring that reserves be held by the clearinghouse for its members as a means of reducing the end-of-day credit risk. Such an innovation might begin as an investigation of the merits of forming a bankers' bank among CHIPS members and requiring collateral or reserves from participants as a prerequisite for settlement. I expect that any such investigation by CHIPS would be short-lived. CHIPS members would probably open their discussions of options to Federal Reserve staff. As long as Corrigan is known to favor Federal Reserve control of CHIPS, the Fed staff would find reasons why a bankers' bank owned by CHIPS participants would not work. Progress would suffer from nitpicking about terms and format. The discussions would no doubt end with a terse announcement by CHIPS that the investigation of settlement alternatives had been postponed.

Expected interference from the Fed would not be the only roadblock. As a practical matter, CHIPS members are unlikely to agree to put up reserves or collateral for settlement rights as long as Fedwire guarantees are free. The current cost of overuse of daylight overdrafts is a memo to the bank's board and perhaps a slap on the wrist for the bank's funds manager. Also, CHIPS reserves are made unnecessary by the fact that if CHIPS members perceive a real risk from another participant, they can use the controls CHIPS already has in place to limit their exposure and force the risky institution to send Fedwires instead of CHIPS payments.

## Pricing Credit Risk

A number of scholarly papers are circulating on the proper pricing of intraday credit, but there has been only limited experimentation with such pricing.[13] To date, experimentation with explicit risk pricing in the private sector has been largely confined to the credit card systems.[14] (For the purposes of this discussion, I ignore the current pricing of CHIPS credit limits[15] and focus on the pricing of risk in the credit card systems.) VISA and MasterCard both employ a pricing method that assesses stores that accept their cards both a per transaction fixed fee and a percentage of the transaction's value to cover the risk of nonpayment in final settlement. In the case of credit cards, the duration of credit risk extends to the cardholder's settlement with the credit card issuer, but the pricing policy nevertheless provides a useful example. The proposed 1989 fee structure on an average bank card transaction value of $60 looks like this: 1.85 percent plus $0.05 = $1.16 for MasterCard and 1.70 percent plus $0.07 = $1.09 for VISA.

Discounts on fees are given for progress toward further automation by participating stores. That is, participants in the credit card market are rewarded for the risk-reducing effects of installing faster, more controlled automated payment systems. The national credit card chains represent systems that have evolved in the private sector in the absence of competition designed by the Federal Reserve. The Fed decided in the late 1960s to stay out of the emerging bank credit card business. In the succeeding 20 years, vigorous competition, leading-edge technology, and the development of an explicitly priced system for the allocation of credit risk have appeared in that market, which seems to work reasonably well.

There might also be a priced credit risk system for check collection today if the Federal Reserve had not eliminated the practice of discounting in check collection some years ago. The Fed staff was convinced that "circuitous routing" and other operating inefficiencies of nonpar check collection created terrible societal burdens, not to mention costs to Federal Reserve Banks. The Federal Reserve's accounts of its war on nonpar check collection usually ignore the fact that the discounts effectively applied a market price to collection float and credit risk. The benefits of market pricing of risks were eliminated in the name of efficiency, or at least to increase the Federal Reserve Banks' share of check collections. If some of the current Federal Reserve Board governors were to reflect on the natural pricing of credit risk that develops in private payment ventures in the absence of Federal Reserve Bank entry, they might discover a policy course that is an alternative to the one that has dominated the payment systems since 1914.

## Current Approaches to Managing Daylight Credit Risk

Despite the increasing attention being given the dangers created by intra-day credit, the Fed continues to maintain that instant guaranteed payment finality is critical to the efficient operation of the payment system. Given the obstinence of the Federal Reserve staff on that point, it might be useful to consider finality more carefully.

In the simplest terms, finality means that a transaction will not be reversed. For example, a Fedwire transfer is said to be final when it is accepted by the Federal Reserve and credited to the account of the receiving institution. The Fed guarantees the settlement of each delivered wire, replacing the credit of the initial sending institution with its own. In the Fed's view, the same-day finality approach is the only way to achieve stability in payments. In my view, the Fed has merely avoided the cost of unwinding a day's transactions and provided a benefit to the Fedwire receiver as a result of its operating decision.

The effect of the Fedwire guarantee is to shift the cost burden of same-day finality to the deposit insurance funds. It was clear in the cases of Continental Illinois and First Republic of Dallas that guaranteed Fedwires produced nothing more than a risk-free emergency withdrawal service for large uninsured depositors and lenders in the overnight market. Large creditors run for the hills at the first sign of a bank's weakness by transferring uninsured balances to other institutions over Fedwire. Such behavior leaves the regional Federal Reserve Bank with a real end-of-day overdraft in the reserve account of the failed institution. But the FDIC's first action after assuming control of a failed bank is to provide ample collateral to the regional Federal Reserve Bank for the overdraft accumulated during the final day before closure. That action by the FDIC is usually ignored by the financial press. Instead of Federal Reserve Board governors explaining to Congress why they guaranteed unsecured transfers by large depositors out of a troubled bank, FDIC officials are chastised for the cost of rescuing a large, illiquid institution.[16] There are no congressional inquiries into the Fed's authority to make unsecured loans or its failure to establish real-time controls on reserve accounts, only questions about the judgment of insurance fund officials.

The bottom-line effect of the Fed's policy on same-day finality is to undermine any efforts by the FDIC to share the costs of a bank failure with the institution's largest creditors. Since the insurance funds are politically less powerful than the Fed because they have no large revenues to pay into the Treasury, they have no choice but to quietly cover the multibillion dollar unsecured credit lines granted by the Federal Reserve Banks and take their lumps from the banking committees and the Independent Bankers Association of America. In the meantime, Federal Reserve officials wring their hands and talk about their valiant, but unsuccessful, attempts to stem the tide in the final days of a failing large bank.[17] The fact that the local Federal Reserve Bank continued to guarantee Fedwires on the final day before the FDIC assumed responsibility for a troubled institution is not reported in the financial press. Having covered the regional reserve banks' unsecured credit lines, the FDIC is rewarded with receivership of an institution with few, if any, uninsured depositors remaining.

### Other Methods of Resolving the Issue

Returning to the volumes of payments (Table 8–2) and shifting the focus of attention to the various kinds of payments, I will argue that some very different approaches to intraday credit risk are necessary. About 50 percent of payments involve the financial investment markets, about 10 percent are traditional payments, and the residual 40 percent are cash management–type transfers. Said another way, 40 percent of the dollars transferred every day have the same party at risk on both ends of the transaction. In addition, finality of wire transfers guarantees that sophisticated uninsured depositors have a Fed guarantee when running on an illiquid institution.

From the details of Table 8–2, it is clear that real commercial payments comprise only a small multiple of reserves, at most three or four times the reserve base. A significant portion of those commercial payments will be nonfinal checks and ACH payments. Meanwhile in the financial markets, major brokers settle securities trades with checks five business days after the trades take place. That gives brokers a week to come up with the cash balance necessary to deal with any major market movements. The Fed has already protected its position in the Treasury securities market. Clearly the bulk of the credit risk involves one-day funds investments and corporate cash management transfers. Why does the Federal Reserve take it upon itself to ensure that overnight lenders and large corporations will be able to withdraw their uninsured deposits at the first sign of financial trouble?

There are alternative policies for dealing with the systemic credit risk currently associated with payments. Indeed, the most important reason for the large volume of transfers made each day is the outmoded regulation of banks themselves. Both the geographic constraints and the limited financial services powers of banks create a multiplication of external transfers unique to the United States.[18]

First, a more national banking system would include fewer total institutions, all of which would have the power to operate branches nationwide. Such consolidation would reduce the number and volume of transfers between banks. Large corporations with widespread offices that must now transfer funds on a daily basis between legally separate banking entities would be able to internalize many transactions within a single bank (e.g., CHIPS volume should decline as a result of the acquisition of Irving by Bankers Trust). Multistate banking can reduce the external transaction volume further by reducing the number of institutions necessary to provide financial services to nationwide businesses.

Second, interest on corporate demand balances would remove another large percentage of the corporate cash concentration transfers from the payment system. Corporate treasurers could leave balances in interest-bearing transaction accounts instead of transferring funds across the country for reinvestment. Even the Fed would benefit from higher reserves on the higher deposit balances.

Finally, payment of market interest on reserve balances could dramatically reduce overnight funds activity, confining activity to necessary borrowing and lending between depositories and eliminating the current scramble among banks to earn marginal returns on excess reserves.

Thus, the current daylight credit exposures are to a large extent a function of outmoded regulation that deprives financial institutions of the ability to expand to serve the needs of a nationwide customer base. The Neanderthal regulations require participants to multiply their transfers from one account to another and from one investment to another. Because implementation of none of the deregulatory approaches to reducing turnover appears to be pending, however, we must consider alternatives that do not require more rational banking laws.

Since the real systemic danger created by illiquid depositories is that other institutions may have balances with them in the normal course of business, we could stop short of fully insuring all deposits in favor of fully insuring only the balances depositories keep with each other. The FDIC and other insurance funds would provide full insurance for every deposit dollar held by one bank for another, and the premium would be charged to the deposit-holding bank. Naturally, the Fed should pay premiums for the reserve balances it holds for other institutions just as any correspondent bank would pay for balances left on deposit. Correspondent fees would rise to cover premiums, and if risk-adjusted premiums ever evolved, the market price would quickly reflect risk. As we saw in the cases of Continental Illinois and First Republic of Dallas, it is the insurance funds that are the true lenders of last resort to the institutions, not the Federal Reserve. The insurance funds should be compensated for the systemic risks they underwrite. I believe Congress would find that approach more attractive than carte blanche insurance for all depositors because the premiums would flow to the insurance funds. Certainly it is more rational than allowing the Fed to charge interest on intraday transactions, depriving the insurance funds of revenue without changing their risk.

The insurance funds could also insure wire transfers. Since the insurance funds are the ultimate guarantors of unsecured Fed credit, they should at least collect the premiums. Of course, the federal insurance funds might also wish to offer wire transfer insurance to private operators who choose to offer same-day final payments. The pricing policy used for retail credit card payments (i.e., transaction fees plus a percentage of the wires) could serve as a model for premiums on transfer insurance, though the rates would probably be lower than on credit cards. Wire transfer insurance would provide additional funding for the deposit insurance funds, and it would presumably eliminate the Fed's policy difficulties with offering settlement to private networks that compete with Fedwire. If wire transfer insurance were adopted, the Fed probably would turn its monitoring of daylight overdrafts into a billing system for the insurance funds. That might create a problem, however, since it seems that the proper premium payor is the receiver of the guaranteed wire, not the initiator.

The deposit insurance funds might also wish to explore an after-hours federal funds market. The insurance funds could pay the Fed to open its Fedwire system for evening trades that would use the insurance funds' guarantee instead of a Federal Reserve guarantee on wires. The overnight wire system would book the terms of the funds traded during regular business hours and credit the borrowing banks' and debit the lending institutions' insured reserve accounts retroactive to close of business on day one; the next day the system would reverse the transaction, collect the interest rate agreed on by the banks, and deduct insurance and transaction fees before turning over the funds to the lending institutions. The insurance funds could guarantee the overnight loan, the return of funds, proper execution of the trade, and the interest payment, which would eliminate both the daylight overdraft and the systemic risk of unreturned overnight loans as well as reduce the current overhead of the overnight funds market. An overnight funds market would unclog the daytime Fedwire network without a capital outlay and maintain the Fed's revenue. The Fed would achieve more daytime Fedwire capacity without capital outlays for upgrading its computers.

The suggestions I have presented obviously need further development to make them fully workable, but they begin to address the questions of who should bear the risk and who would benefit from a more rational environment for guaranteed payments. In my view, the ultimate guarantor of funds transfers is the deposit insurance system, and that system should also be the beneficiary of premiums paid for its guarantees.

## Notes

1. A "repo" is a repurchase agreement for securities that has the effect of a collateralized borrowing at an agreed rate for a fixed term.

2. The estimate that 75 percent of overnight transactions are accounted for by the federal funds market comes from an undated memo by David Humphrey of the Richmond Federal Reserve Bank.

3. Indeed, if you look at the series for all banks (A 18), the number disappears, presumably because the lending banks cancel out the borrowing ones.

4. The multiplier of 10 is my own estimate of the complex market structure in the United States. I believe that multiplier overestimates commercial transactions and thus reduces the value of transfers (discussed later) to a more conservative level than would a lower multiplier. Using 10 also makes the actual daily average values obvious because no complex calculations are required.

5. The classic example of cash management uses the Southland Corporation's 7-Eleven Stores to illustrate the most common service. Each store opens its own local bank account and permits Southland to draw against it. The stores deposit their receipts daily and report their deposits to central bookkeeping using a special telephone number. Bookkeeping prepares debits that draw down the stores' balances, and the funds are then credited to Southland's account, thus "concentrating" the receipts for corporate investment or funding accounts payable. Both paper and electronic debit services are available from a variety of commercial banks. The service is often tailored to the specific funding needs of the corporate treasurer. Such cash management practices are typical of national and regional corporations faced with branch-banking restrictions.

6. My own view is that clearinghouses were established by progressive bank management

who saw the advantages of hub-and-spoke transportation networks for package deliveries well before Federal Express was invented. Gorton (1984) provides a more academic discussion of the topic.

7. Gorton's (1984) article provides a good summary of those developments. For a more detailed treatment of the early history of clearinghouses, see Cannon (1905).

8. Values for New York were provided to the author by the New York Clearing House Association. Values for other cities are based on Dun and Bradstreet's (1988) report of weekly clearing totals divided by five. Dun and Bradstreet discontinued publication of *Bank Clearings* in mid-1988. Current weekly clearing reports are published jointly by Martin D. Weiss Research, Inc., and T. J. Hold & Co. in the subscription newsletter *Business Forecasts*.

9. Lenders to the overnight federal funds market follow that pattern. Those lenders like to get their money back early and then take their time shopping the market before recommitting the funds later in the day. Dealers in government securities also frequently accumulate large blocks of securities before selling the block. As they build their securities positions, the dealers owe large cash balances. When they move the block later in the day, the credit flows back to them.

10. Clair (1991) details the types of caps and their history.

11. Since bank examinations are largely the work of the comptroller of the currency, state banking departments, the FDIC, and the Federal Home Loan Banks, those agencies bear the cost of seeing that the caps are adhered to. Such monitoring diverts the attention of bank examiners from other supervisory activities or increases the resources expended on supervision. It is interesting to note that the Federal Home Loan Banks do not permit their member institutions to run *any* Fed daylight overdrafts. Clearly, the Federal Home Loan Banks have more significant problems with which to deal than Federal Reserve daylight overdrafts.

12. It is interesting to note that though the Fed has required private systems to install real-time monitors to limit intraday credit abuses, Fedwire has yet to install them across its entire system.

13. In fact, the Federal Reserve Bank of Richmond hosted a two-day symposium on the payment system in May 1988.

14. See, for example, Kutler (1988a and 1988b). Kutler concerns himself with other aspects of card transaction processing, but the data are sufficient to provide a view of two competing explicitly priced credit risk allocation systems.

15. The credit limits CHIPS participants impose on each other are a form of pricing. If a bank wishes to send CHIPS payments to Morgan, it must negotiate a line of credit from Morgan to cover the value of those transactions net of any Morgan transfers to the first bank. Each CHIPS payment the bank sends uses up a portion of its credit line until it is offset by a Morgan CHIPS payment to the first bank. CHIPS payments cost the bank transaction fees and the cost of using its line of credit at whatever price it negotiated for its credit arrangement at Morgan. The credit line cost may take the form of fees or required correspondent balances that have a cost in marginal investment value lost to the bank.

16. Congressional hearings and media coverage usually confuse depositors' insurance with the interests of the owners and managers of the bank. How the liquidation of the owners' interests, the termination of senior management, the repayment of the overdraft at the local Fed, and the payment of claims of insured depositors came to be known as "bailout" or "rescue" of the failed bank remains a mystery.

17. The Chicago Fed's balance sheet, congressional hearings on Continental Illinois, and the contemporary financial press support that interpretation.

18. Hollis (1990) expressed similar views at the Richmond Fed's symposium. The topic was float, but my thoughts on payment risk were influenced by his remarks.

# References

Cannon, James G. 1905. *Clearinghouses*. New York: D. Appleton and Company.

Clair, Robert T. 1991. "Daylight Overdrafts: Who Really Bears the Risk?" Chapter 8 in this book.

Corrigan, E. Gerald. 1987. "Financial Market Structure: A Longer View." Federal Reserve Bank of New York *Annual Report*, pp. 3–54.

Dun and Bradstreet. 1988. *Bank Clearings*. New York: Dun and Bradstreet.

Federal Reserve Board. 1988a. "Electronic Clearinghouse Study." Report to Congress, May, appendix B.

Federal Reserve Board. 1988b. "Financial and Business Statistics." *Federal Reserve Bulletin* 74, no. 8 (August).

Gorton, Gary. 1984. "Private Clearinghouses and the Origins of Central Banking." Federal Reserve Bank of Philadelphia *Business Review* (January/February): 3–12.

Hollis, Donald R. 1990. "Commentary." In *The U.S. Payment System: Efficiency, Risk, and the Role of the Federal Reserve*, proceedings of a symposium on the U.S. payment system sponsored by the Federal Reserve Bank of Richmond, May 25–26, 1988, edited by David B. Humphrey, pp. 87–92. Boston: Kluwer Academic Publishers.

Humphrey, David B. Undated. "Determining the Impact of Daily Federal Funds Transactions on Daylight Overdrafts." Memorandum to the Federal Reserve Board of Governors.

Kutler, Jeffrey. 1988a. "Card Pricing Dispute Escalates." *American Banker*, September 30, p. 1.

Kutler, Jeffrey. 1988b. "Complex Pricing Mechanism Underlies Card Industry Flap." *American Banker*, September 30, p. 14.

# 9 THE GOVERNMENT'S ROLE IN PAYMENT SYSTEMS: LESSONS FROM THE CANADIAN EXPERIENCE

Angela Redish

Technological and ideological changes have encouraged a reexamination of the regulation of the financial sector in many Western economies, and the regulation of payment services has constituted an important component of that study. Although payment services are used by all economic agents, the details of their functions are not widely understood. Yet an understanding of the current payment system is necessary if improvements are to be instituted. Understanding the payment systems of other nations and other times is also important; although economic theory can suggest the effects of a changing environment, those other systems are the only sources of laboratory-type results. This paper uses historical and contemporary Canadian experience to help illustrate the costs and benefits of government intervention in the payment system.

Goodfriend and King (1988) divide the functions of the central bank

The author is an associate professor in the Department of Economics of the University of British Columbia, Vancouver, Canada. She would like to thank Michael Bordo, James Dingle, Catherine England, and Ronald Shearer for useful comments. All errors and omissions remain the author's responsibility.

into monetary policy (those functions that necessarily involve changing the stock of high-powered money) and banking policy (those functions that focus on the regulation and supervision of the banking sector). For example, they argue that central bank lending to an individual bank is banking policy, while central bank lending in the face of a systemwide liquidity crisis is monetary policy.[1] In addition to setting the central bank's banking policy, the government's role in the payment system, at least potentially, includes the issue of notes and the activities of regulatory agencies other than the central bank, including the deposit insurance agency, and the clearinghouses.

The first half of this paper is an overview of the historical and contemporary role of the government in the Canadian payment system. The second part examines the implications of that experience for theoretical analyses of the necessity for government intervention. Few general conclusions emerge. In both Canada and the United States, direct government involvement increased at least until the late 1970s, and permanent institutional changes have frequently resulted from temporary problems. In Canada the government's role in the payment system is less than it is in the United States. Yet the high degree of concentration in the banking sector means that the Canadian experience cannot be used to illustrate the effects of private firms' competing to offer payment services through the marketplace. The Canadian experience does, however, show that alternative institutional structures can offer efficient payment services.

## The Evolution of the Canadian Payment System

Five areas of Canadian banking policy have been selected for discussion: the issue of high-powered money, the regulation and supervision of banks, the operation of clearinghouses, the function of the lender of last resort, and the insurance of bank liabilities.

### Currency

In early 19th-century Canada, the primary role of the monetary authorities was to define a numeraire. They did so by giving unit-of-account values to foreign coins, the sole legal tender and the primary medium of exchange at the time. The first Canadian banks opened in the 1820s, and bank notes and checks drawn on deposits became the dominant means of payment, although gold coin remained the only legal tender. In 1860, in response to a fiscal crisis, the goverment began issuing its own monetary liabilities, which were called Provincial notes before confederation in 1867 and Dominion notes thereafter. In 1935 the Bank of Canada was established, and Bank of Canada notes and deposits replaced Dominion notes.

Initially, Dominion notes circulated in competition with private bank issues. However, after 1870 the government obtained a monopoly over the issue of notes of less than $5 (i.e., denominations of $1, $2, and $4). Dominion notes were then virtually confined to those small bills and large-denomination bills of $500, $1,000, and $5,000, called "large legals," that were primarily used as reserves by the banks. After 1944 private notes were gradually retired, and the Bank of Canada acquired a monopoly over the issue of all notes.

## Regulation and Supervision

In the early years of Canadian banking there were only a few regulations, but they were quite significant. Banks were required to obtain a charter from the colonial government in order to obtain limited liability status. Charters typically restricted lending to "real bills" (i.e., short-term commercial loans) and restricted the amount of notes issued to less than the amount of paid-in capital. A high minimum paid-in capital requirement restricted entry into the industry. Noticeably absent were restrictions on the opening of branches and any government-specified level of required reserves. The banks were required to supply balance sheet data to the government annually, and they were bound by usury laws that prohibited their charging interest rates greater than 6 percent.

The extent of regulation has fluctuated over the past 150 years, but two characteristics of the system remain largely unchanged: the highly concentrated nature of the banking system and a reliance on self-regulation. Until the 1960s regulation encouraged the separation and independence of the four sectors of the financial industry—banking, insurance, trusts, and securities brokerage—commonly called the "four pillars" of the Canadian financial sector. But by 1962 the distinctions among the four sectors were becoming blurred, and near-banks were offering many services that competed with bank products. Trust companies, credit unions, and (in Quebec) *caisses populaires* all offered checking and savings accounts.[2] Since those near-banks competitors were not subject to the costs imposed on banks by usury laws, reserve requirements, and lending restrictions, they could offer more attractive interest rates on deposits. In 1962 the

Royal Commission on Banking and Finance (widely known as the Porter commission) recommended steps that would increase competition in the financial sector and unify the regulatory structure. The introduction of a unified system of regulation has been foiled primarily by the problem of competing jurisdictions: banks and some trust companies are under federal jurisdiction, while other trust companies, credit unions, and *caisses populaires* come under provincial jurisdiction.

The primary vehicle for regulatory change over the past 150 years has been the decennial revision of the Bank Act.[3] The 1870 Bank Act renewed all bank charters for 10 years, and since then decennial renewals have been used to review and amend bank legislation. The security against which banks may lend has gradually been broadened from real bills. (Significant recent steps include the right to fund insured mortgages in 1954 and to make all types of mortgage loans in 1967.) In addition, the 1967 Bank Act revision removed the interest rate ceiling on bank loans. The introduction of required reserves in 1935 added to the restrictions faced by banks and hence offset liberalizing changes to some degree, although in recent years the reserve requirements have been reduced (to reduce the competitive advantage of nonbank depository institutions not subject to reserve requirements).

Before 1980 there were few changes in the restrictions on entry into the banking sector. Firms seeking to establish banks had to obtain a bank charter by a special act of Parliament and had to have minimum subscribed capital of $1 million. There were also limitations on foreign ownership and on the extent of any one individual's ownership of a bank. The 1980 Bank Act significantly reduced the barriers to entry by permitting banks to incorporate under letters patent (i.e., upon written application to the minister of finance and compliance with the criteria specified in the act) instead of by a special act of Parliament. In addition, the act introduced a second category of banks known as Schedule B banks, not subject to the restrictions on narrow ownership and ownership by foreigners that Schedule A banks face. However, Schedule B banks are only permitted one branch (unless they obtain permission from the minister of finance), require a minimum capital of $2.5 million if they are foreign owned, and must limit assets to 20 times capital. To date the 1980 legislation has had only a slight impact on concentration in the banking sector. On June 30, 1988, the "Big 5" Canadian banks held 83 percent of industry assets,[4] and foreign-owned banks held less than 10 percent of industry assets. On June 30, 1980, the Big 5 banks held 90 percent of industry assets.

Calls for external inspection of banks date from at least the 1880s, but it was not until the failure of the Home Bank in 1923 that the government created the Office of the Inspector General of Banks and required annual bank inspections. Even today bank inspection and monitoring are conducted on a scale vastly different from that on which they are conducted in the United States. There is a tripartite inspection process.[5] Each bank has internal audit procedures, the objectives of which are to prevent fraud and to monitor the behavior of bank officers. Banks are also externally audited by an audit company whose responsibility is to assure the shareholders (and other interested parties) that the banks' financial statements correctly reflect their financial position in accordance with generally accepted accounting principles as modified by the Bank Act. Finally, the Superintendant of Financial Institutions (the SFI replaced the OIGB in July 1987) does its own inspection. Those three levels are not, however, independent. The external auditors rely on the reports of the internal auditors, and the SFI relies on the external auditors' reports. Indeed, with a staff of 21 (in 1986) to monitor all banks, it is hard to see how the SFI could do otherwise.

## The Clearinghouses

The first clearinghouse in Canada began operations in Halifax in 1887, and shortly thereafter clearinghouses opened in Montreal and Toronto. The Montreal clearinghouse reportedly reduced the time required for daily exchange, freed cash, and reduced the risk to bank messengers (Denison 1967 p. 242). Sixteen banks joined the Montreal clearinghouse when it opened, and on the first day of operation, checks and notes worth roughly $1.5 million were settled in 50 minutes with $400,000 in cash.

In 1900 the Canadian Bankers' Association began operating the clearinghouses. The CBA was formed in 1890 as an industry association to promote the interests of the banks by publishing a quarterly journal and training officers, for example. The CBA managed the clearinghouses, but the actual clearing was done at a selected bank in each city. The CBA set the rules and adjudicated disputes. Initially, settlement was done through balances held by each bank at the local clearing bank. After 1926 statements of balances were sent from each clearing point to Montreal and net balances were settled there. Before 1935, settlement was usually made in large legals. After the establishment of the Bank of Canada, settlement was made by debits and credits to each bank's account at that bank.

The Porter commission argued in 1962 that the clearing system handicapped near-banks that wished to compete in the deposit business. Near-banks had to employ a chartered bank to act as their clearing agent. In

1976 the "White Paper on the Revision of Canadian Banking Legislation" (Canada, Department of Finance, 1976) recommended that a new clearing system, to which all deposit-taking firms could belong, be established. In 1980 the Canadian Payments Association was formed with a mandate to "broaden the membership of the clearing system and to ensure orderly planning of payments systems development" (Canada, Department of Finance, 1978, p. 2). It took over the operation of the clearing system in November 1983.

The CPA consists of 140 members including chartered banks, credit union centrals, trust and loan companies, and the Bank of Canada. All Schedule A banks are required to be members of the CPA, and most are direct clearers. Other financial institutions may join the CPA, and if their volume of clearing items is at least ½ of 1 percent of the national total they may become direct clearers.[6] Other members operate as indirect clearers as described below. In addition to supervising the daily clearing and settlement process, the association has a senior planning committee that is currently developing a point-of-sale electronic funds transfer system and is also examining methods of providing a separate large-value (over $50,000) transfer system (Canadian Payments Association 1988).

Each direct clearer operates a data center at each of eight regional locations, and all items to be cleared are sent to the nearest data center. Items to be cleared are divided into intrainstitutional (about a quarter of the total) and interinstitutional. The clearing process is most easily described by an example. Imagine that on November 1 Ms. A deposits a check at her Vancouver branch of the Royal Bank. It is a check drawn by Mr. B on his Ottawa branch of the Bank of Montreal. Both banks are direct clearers. Ms. A is given provisional credit by the Royal Bank. She will earn interest from November 1, and may (depending on individual bank practice) be permitted immediate access to the funds, on the understanding that she will have to repay the bank if Mr. B's check is returned. At the end of the day the Royal Bank sends the check to its data center where it is encoded and added to the parcel of items for exchange with the Bank of Montreal. The total of that parcel of claims is entered into the CPA's automated clearing and settlement system (the ACSS) later that evening. The Royal Bank sends the parcel of items to the Bank of Montreal data center in Vancouver where its contents are verified. The account of Mr. B is then debited, and the check is forwarded by the Bank of Montreal to its Ottawa branch. At 9:30 a.m. November 2 the ACSS is closed to further entries, and that afternoon the Bank of Canada determines the clearing balances of each direct clearer. Those amounts are then debited or credited to each bank's deposit at the Bank of Canada.

The entries are, however, backdated to the previous business day, in this case November 1.[7]

Let us now consider the nature of balances kept by direct clearers at the Bank of Canada. The direct clearers can be divided into the nine Schedule A chartered banks, which account for 76 percent of the clearing volume, and the others. The direct clearers, both banks and nonbanks, are required to maintain deposit accounts with the Bank of Canada. Those accounts are debited or credited as a result of the clearings. All direct clearers have access to a line of credit (that is, to the discount window) at the Bank of Canada equal to 2.5 percent of their checkable deposits. Advances under the line of credit are against promissory notes of the borrowing institution secured by any of a wide range of collateral, usually government securities.

Indirect clearers do not have accounts at the Bank of Canada; instead they hold clearing balances at one of the direct clearers. An indirect clearer will send all its items to be cleared to the nearest data center of its clearing affiliate, who will credit the account of the indirect clearer and then send the items for settlement with its own items. The direct clearer establishes a line of credit for its affiliate and is required to report to the regulatory authorities if the indirect clearer obtains extraordinary advances (i.e., advances in excess of its line of credit) on more than two business days in any month.

Let us turn now to the problem of default risk and the issue of who bears the costs if an institution fails or becomes insolvent.[8] Significantly, the CPA itself bears no liability. The risks are borne by the direct clearers. Consider first the effect of default by a direct clearer. Suppose, referring to the earlier example, that at 9:30 a.m. November 2 the Bank of Montreal has a debit balance that exceeds its deposit at the Bank of Canada inclusive of any advance granted on its line of credit. The Bank of Montreal is in default and is required to return through the clearinghouse all items it received that are still in its possession. There is then a new accounting at the clearinghouse to eliminate the returned items. If the defaulting institution is a clearing agent for an indirect clearer with a clearing loss for the day, the affiliate is required to deposit funds at the Bank of Canada to cover the amount it owes its clearing agent.

In the simplest case, there are no new defaulters, and the system clears. Those holding claims against the defaulting institution proceed as unsecured creditors. Two possible problems may emerge. A complete unwind may not be possible because frequently some of the paper has already been cleared. For example, if the check written by Mr. B has already been cleared and is given to Mr. B at 8:00 a.m. on November 2, that transaction cannot be unwound. If the Bank of Montreal were still in default after all possible transactions were unwound, the other direct clearers would be required to lend funds to the defaulting institution so that the defaulter had a balance sufficient to settle the remaining items. Such loans are made by the direct clearers to whom the defaulter is a debtor, and each must lend "in proportion to the amounts which are due to them."[9]

The second difficulty that could emerge is that after the first unwind (and possible forced loans) there may be another institution in default. That is the case of systemic risk, which Humphrey (1986) has analyzed in the context of the Clearing House Interbank Payment System. The Canadian clearing system is similar to CHIPS and therefore faces systemic risk. But such risk does not seem to be a major problem. The Bank of Canada has an obligation to lend to illiquid banks that are not insolvent, so that if a second institution became illiquid because of a default by one institution, the second illiquid bank would be able to borrow from the Bank of Canada. The fact that there are only 13 (other than the Bank of Canada) direct clearers makes the operation of the discount window easier than it would be if there were thousands of banks. If the supervisory system is functioning properly, systemic risk should be negligible.

The case of the default of an indirect clearer is slightly different. If an indirect clearer is in default, its clearing affiliate returns all items and the direct clearers have "whatever remedies are provided by law against prior parties to such items." [10]

In law, therefore, the CPA bears no default risk, and the Bank of Canada's risk is limited to its liability as a direct clearer. The risk is borne by the individual members of the CPA. Each member of the CPA therefore has an interest in the solvency of other members, yet the CPA has no power to refuse membership or to inspect its members.[11] However, access to the payment system is restricted to institutions that have guaranteed deposits and are subject to inspection by federal or provincial regulatory authorities. That is necessary (according to the chairman of the CPA) to preserve the integrity of the system and to "prevent failures as far as possible but also to preserve the basis of mutual trust that underlies the efficient operation of the system" (Vachon 1987, p. 10).

A significant difference between the Canadian payment system and that of the United States is the absence of a special clearing mechanism for large-value payments. In 1987 paper items over $50,000 in value made up 92.4 percent of the value of cleared items and 0.34 percent of the volume (Anvari 1990, p. 12). The clearing and settlement of large-value items is a focus of current planning efforts by the CPA, which is examining alternative systems that would provide faster clearing and finality of payment for such items. It seems likely that whatever changes are made, the CPA will maintain the principle of allowing the Bank of Canada and the CPA to bear no risk. The two alternatives then are to allow no daylight overdrafts or to require clearing institutions to insure against default.

## The Lender of Last Resort

Until 1907 there was no lender of last resort in Canada. During the crisis of 1907 the government issued and lent to the banks (possibly illegally) $5 million Dominion notes that were repaid within six months. World War I intervened before any permanent machinery evolved. The sudden cessation of capital imports at the onset of the war created expectations that Canada would be unable to maintain its fixed exchange rate, and the subsequent run on the banks was halted by the suspension of gold convertibility of Dominion notes and legislation (the Finance Act) that permitted banks to borrow Dominion notes from the Finance Department. The convertibility of Dominion notes was restored in 1926, but the Finance Act, intended only for wartime, was amended and made permanent in 1923. In 1935 the Bank of Canada took over from the Finance Department the operation of the discount window.

Use of the discount window has varied enormously. In 1929 banks borrowed considerable sums from the government because the rate charged by the Finance Department was less than the New York interest rate. In February 1929 the minister of finance suspended the unrestricted convertibility of Dominion notes, thereby removing the incentive for banks to borrow Dominion notes to obtain gold for investing in New York.

Currently, the Bank of Canada lends for two reasons. Overnight loans are used when banks need overnight funds, often because a clearing loss leaves them short of their required reserves. Emergency loans can be used for up to six months and are renewable. Those loans are available to institutions considered solvent but illiquid. The SFI is responsible for assessing the solvency of banks. If the SFI states that an institution is insolvent, a curator is appointed to liquidate its assets. Use of the Bank of Canada's discount window varies considerably; some banks never borrow and others routinely use the discount window. Martin (1985, p. 27) states that one of the larger Canadian banks was reported "to have taken great pride in never having asked for a cash advance from the Bank of Canada."

The Bank of Canada has no inspection or supervisory powers and relies on the reports of the SFI. All direct clearers have access to a line of credit with the Bank of Canada, and other depository institutions can obtain emergency funds from the Canada Deposit Insurance Corporation.

## Note and Deposit Insurance

Deposit insurance is a relatively recent development in Canada. The Canada Deposit Insurance Corporation was established by the 1967 revision of the Bank Act, but an insurance system for notes issued by chartered banks was established as early as 1890. The Bank Circulation Redemption Fund required all chartered banks to pay in 5 percent of their circulation (McIvor 1961, p. 77). The fund was held by the minister of finance and paid interest at 3 percent on reserves. Before the BCRF was established, note holders had first claim on the assets of an insolvent bank when it was liquidated, but obtaining payment was a slow and uncertain process. The BCRF reimbursed note holders immediately and thereby prevented the depreciation of notes of insolvent banks. Bank liquidators were then required to pay an amount to the fund equal to the amount of notes redeemed before the proceeds of the asset sales could be distributed to other creditors.

The CDIC was established with a mandate to provide insurance to small depositors and to minimize the losses associated with failures (Canada Deposit Insurance Corporation 1986). The CDIC is a government-owned crown corporation that guarantees all bank and many near-bank deposits up to a maximum of $60,000 per account. The banks originally argued that deposit insurance was not necessary and that, if it were instituted, premiums should be related to risk. Neither of those arguments was successful.

In 1987 the CDIC had 67 bank members, 58 federal trust and loan company members, and 37 provincial trust and loan company members. The corporation's funds come from flat-rate premiums levied at a rate of $1/10$ of 1 percent of insurable deposits. (The rate was increased in 1986 from $1/30$ of 1 percent.) In the first 16 years of its existence, the corporation was involved with only 4 terminations, but between 1983 and 1987, there were 18 instances in which the corporation was required to honor its obligation as an insurer—including 3 bank-related events.

The CDIC either liquidates an insolvent member or institutes an agency agreement.[12] When the corporation undertakes an agency agreement, it effectively protects all depositors (not just explicitly insured depositors). In 1984 the corporation noted "the adverse effect that the mere perception that such a [full payout] policy exists may have on market discipline" and emphasized that an agency agreement is only instituted where "it reduces a potential risk or the threat of a loss" (Canada Deposit Insurance Corporation 1984, p. 7).

To date, in the three instances in which banks were in difficulty, all depositors were fully compensated.[13] The first bank failures in Canada since 1923 occurred in 1985 when the Canadian Commercial Bank and the Northland Bank went into receivership. When the Canadian Commercial Bank told a meeting of various monetary authorities in March 1985 that it was insolvent, a bailout was arranged. Six of the larger Canadian banks joined the CDIC in buying part of the bank's portfolio for $255 million. The CDIC's share was $75 million. However, that help was insufficient, and the bank closed its doors six months later, as did a second western Canadian bank, the Northland Bank. The government passed special legislation to compensate the uninsured depositors of both banks.[14] Although the payments were implemented by the CDIC, the funds did not come out of its budget but from general government revenue. The CDIC was also involved in 1986 when the Bank of British Columbia was sold to the Hong Kong Bank of Canada. The CDIC contributed $200 million to the deal, "for purposes of reducing a risk or averting a threatened loss to the Corporation" (Canada Deposit Insurance Corporation 1986, p. 19).

The CDIC has the authority to inspect members annually, but the SFI inspects federally incorporated institutions and provincial regulators inspect provincially incorporated institutions on behalf of the CDIC.

## Is Intervention Necessary?

Let us turn now to the lessons to be learned from this survey of the role of government in the Canadian payment system.

### Currency

Why does the Bank of Canada hold a monopoly over note issue? The historical evidence shows that the first government issues were aimed neither at providing a medium of exchange (which was satisfactorily done by private institutions) nor at conducting monetary policy (which was unnecessary in the gold standard era) but at capturing some seigniorage revenue. Thus, a possible justification of the government's behavior is that seigniorage is a relatively efficient source of government revenue. That probably made more sense in the mid-19th century than it does in the late 20th century.

Perhaps surprisingly, one justification for restrictions on private note issues came from Adam Smith. Smith (1978, p. 422) recommended a prohibition on the issue of notes of less than five pounds,[15] arguing that if small notes are permitted, many mean people are enabled and encouraged to become bankers. A person whose promisory note for five pounds, or even for twenty shillings would be rejected by everybody, will get it to be received without scruple when it is issued for so small a sum as sixpence. But the frequent bankruptcies to which such beggarly bankers must be liable may occasion a very considerable inconveniency, and sometimes even a very great calamity to many poor people who had received their notes in payment.

The Canadian experience with note issue in the 19th and early 20th centuries does not support Smith's concern. His analysis could, however, be read as a justification for deposit insurance for small depositors.

It is important to emphasize that even after the abandonment of the gold standard (and indeed even in the absence of reserve requirements), the government's conduct of monetary policy does not require that government-issued notes be in circulation. Monetary policy can operate successfully as long as the demand for high-powered money exists, and a demand for reserves is a sufficient condition for that.

### Regulation and Supervision

There are several, possibly complementary, justifications for regulating and monitoring banks, but none of them finds complete support in Canadian experience. The first is that the oligopolistic nature of the banking system implies a need for regulation. The second suggests that efficient regulation may improve the efficiency of the banking industry. Finally, it is argued that the operators of a lender-of-last-resort facility and of deposit insurance need to have regulatory and supervisory power.

If economies of scale were the source of the oligopolistic structure of the banking system, a prima facie case could be made for regulation of the industry. However, the evidence suggests that the sources of the oligopolistic structure are to be found in the regulatory environment rather than in economies of scale.[16] Near-banks are considerably smaller than banks. While the mean value of the assets of the domestic banks is $44.9 billion,[17] the mean level of assets of the more than 3,000 credit unions is only $14.09 million. As noted above, it is costly to obtain a charter for a Schedule A bank. For example, the minimum subscribed capital of a chartered bank is $1 million, which must be paid in within one year of incorporation. [National banks in the United States have minimum capital requirements in the $50,000 to $200,000 range (Shearer, Chant, and Bond 1984, p. 358)].

If scale economies were the motive for regulation, one might expect regulation to control prices, restrict profits, and increase output. That is the sort of regulation observed in the public utilities industries in which economies of scale lead to industry concentration. The regulation of the banking sector is not of that kind.

An alternative and more sophisticated argument for regulation has been put forward by Chant (1987), who argues that regulation can improve efficiency in an industry by expanding the range of contracts parties can undertake in an environment of costly and imperfect information flows. Regulation may enable parties to make credible commitments and may be preferable to going to court for remedial action. Chant argues that individuals hold bank deposits (i.e., deposits with fixed rather than floating values) because it reduces their need to monitor the behavior of the banks at the margin, since all the marginal benefits flow to the bank. To put it another way, if a bank manages its portfolio particularly well, it gains all the extra income earned. Therefore a bank has a financial incentive to manage its portfolio (which is in fact the funds that depositors have lent it) as well as possible, and a depositor does not have to personally check up on his bank's portfolio management. However, if a bank incurs large losses, its depositors will lose some or all of their deposits, so depositors must still be concerned with global incentives. Chant (1987, p. 67) notes that the incentive structure is such that

1.  financial institutions might wish to hold riskier assets than would be desired by their depositors;
2.  financial institutions might invest more in equity relative to debt than would be in the interests of their depositors;
3.  the operators of financial institutions might have an incentive to misappropriate resources from the financial institution against the interests of depositors.

Those problems, inherent in private contracts, suggest that efficient regulations would restrict the kinds of assets a bank could hold and the organizational structures of banks.

That argument is appealing and internally consistent, and it does predict the type of regulation observed in the Canadian banking industry. However, the history of Canadian bank regulation cannot be explained solely by such a model. For example, the model suggests that individual banks might not wish to be open about their operations or restrict their asset structures without a credible commitment from their competitors to do the same. It also suggests that they would all gain if they did so. Yet banks have continually and successfully fought against the external inspections that can ensure that all institutions play by the same rules. As the Estey (1986) inquiry forcefully noted, the supervision of banks relies primarily on the banks' internal monitoring systems. That is inconsistent with the efficient regulation model.

The argument that a monetary authority needs regulatory and supervisory power because it acts as a lender of last resort or deposit insurer has two parts: Are lender of last resort and deposit insurer necessarily roles for the government? If so, do they imply a need for regulation and supervision? I focus on the latter question here and examine the former in the next two subsections.

Goodfriend and King (1988) argue that a lender of last resort must be able to determine when a bank is illiquid but not insolvent. They define the problem faced by a lender of last resort as follows: Assume that there is a pool of banks, some strong and some weak, and that an individual bank applies to borrow funds. If the soundness of the bank cannot be determined, the bank can borrow funds at a rate $(r^*)$; if the bank is identified as sound, it can borrow at a lower rate $(r')$. Goodfriend and King define as illiquid but not insolvent a bank that would have a positive net worth if it borrowed at $r'$ but a negative net worth if it borrowed at $r^*$. Lenders of last resort must be able to identify such banks, and since the need for funds is typically immediate, they must monitor banks continuously in order to be able to provide immediate funds. (Goodfriend and King argue that that is completely analogous to the behavior of a private bank that gives a firm a line of credit.)

Again, although the argument is internally consistent and may provide an explanation of the present monitoring activities of the monetary authorities, the historical evidence does not support it as an explanation of the development of the current regulatory system. The discount window began operations in 1914 before any bank inspections were required. Bank inspections resulted from public outcry after the collapse of a mid-sized bank. It was depositors—in the era before deposit insurance—rather than the lender of last resort who demanded governmental supervision. Today the Bank of Canada is the lender of last resort, and a branch of the Department of Finance is responsible for the supervision of banks. That is not to deny the force of the Goodfriend and King argument, but it suggests that the need for a lender of last resort to monitor banks on an ongoing basis is not the only reason for supervisory and regulatory activities. That conclusion is significant because Goodfriend and King go on to argue that a lender of last resort is unnecessary, which implies that supervision is unnecessary.

The requirement that all banks belong to the CDIC and its practice of charging a flat-rate fee imply that banks have an incentive to hold a riskier portfolio than they would if they (or their depositors) had to pay the full price of that risk. As O'Driscoll (1988, p. 168) notes, "Moral hazard occurs when the provision of insurance itself diminishes the incentives facing the insured to avoid risk, thereby increasing the occurence insured against." Regulation and supervision can be a substitute for those incentives. Interestingly, there was little change in the regulatory process in 1967 when the CDIC was introduced, from which I conclude that the regulation of banks in Canada is not founded on correcting the incentives distorted by the nature of deposit insurance.

### The Clearinghouses

The clearinghouses that operated in the United States before 1914 typically broadened their functions and, through the issue of clearinghouse certificates during banking crises, acted as a form of deposit insurance or lender of last resort (Gorton 1985). Although there is little evidence on the historical behavior of the Canadian clearinghouses, it seems that they played a much narrower role; they performed only the clearing and settlement function. Gorton's (1985) argument that the clearinghouse enabled banks to "act as a single firm" during panics may explain the different evolution of the Canadian clearinghouses. In Canada with its branch-banking system, the branches actually did belong to larger banks so there was no need to find organizational ways to get around legislation that prescribed unit banks. The dependence on unit banking in the United States may have led the government to feel it was necessary to undertake the ancillary roles of the clearinghouse while Canadian clearing arrangements remained in private hands.

The operations of the Fedwire system shed more light on the issue. Agents that use Fedwire are permitted free daylight overdrafts that allow them to effect speedy payments with finality.[18] However, the dollar value of the transactions is so large that only the Fed can offer such overdraft facilities (i.e., only the Fed can credibly guarantee that all transactions will be settled). Thus, while the Bank of Canada is not as exposed to risk as is the Fed, it has a slower payment system for large-value items. A private clearinghouse could not operate a system that allowed such large overdrafts.

### Lender of Last Resort

Goodfriend and King (1988, p. 14) argue that there is no need for the monetary authority to act as a lender of last resort to an individual bank that is illiquid but not insolvent.[19] "The efficiency of discount window lending turns on the relative efficiency of the government and the private sector in undertaking a productive activity [distinguishing between illiquid and insolvent banks]." They argue that there is no evidence that the government is better at that activity than is the private sector and that the government's difficulty in refusing to lend to insolvent banks may put it at a disadvantage.

That argument is not strong. When banks that provide line-of-credit services to nonbanks monitor their clients on an ongoing basis, they are not simultaneously obtaining information on how a competitor is performing. That would be the case, however, if banks provided line-of-credit services to each other. In addition, Canadian experience does not support the view that the lender of last resort would have to bail out insolvent banks. When the Canadian Commercial Bank became insolvent in 1985, the Bank of Canada ceased lending to it. The decision of the Canadian government to bail out the bank was completely separate from the Bank of Canada's functions as lender of last resort. It was a political decision that reflected concern about the electorate in the western part of the country and a lack of experience with bank insolvencies. But there is no reason to believe the CCB would not have been bailed out if liquidity advances had been made available only through private sources.

### Deposit Insurance

O'Driscoll argues for a transition from government-sponsored deposit insurance to private deposit insurance to reduce the moral hazard problems inherent in the current system and thereby the need to regulate the banking system. He argues that an unregulated private banking system would have banks that were more diversified, and therefore stronger, and that the system would be more likely to internalize the costs of individual bank failures, which would otherwise generate negative externalities for the system. He uses Canadian experience during the 1930s to illustrate the strength of a diversified banking system and the experience of the Canadian Commercial Bank to illustrate the ability of banks to internalize the externalities of bank failures: "Recognizing that all would suffer from the spread of the contagion effect, the stronger institutions were prepared to lend on the value of the sound assets of the weaker institutions" (O'Driscoll 1988, p. 176). Unfortunately his use of the Canadian evidence is inappropriately selective.

It is certainly true that Canadian experience during the Great Depression showed the advantages of a concentrated system of nationwide branch banks. Those banks—which could diversify both their loans and their deposits—were stronger than unit banks in the United States. But, as O'Driscoll notes, the concentration in the Canadian banking industry was largely due to barriers to entry.[20] It was precisely when competition in the system increased, as barriers to entry fell and competition from near-banks became more important, that Canadians felt it necessary to introduce deposit insurance. Canadian experience has not been with an unregulated banking system but with a banking system that has a particular set of regulations.

The use of the bailout of the Canadian Commercial Bank to demonstrate how bank failures would be internalized in the absence of deposit insurance is also interesting. The CDIC was a major contributor to the bailout package, and there is no evidence that the bailout would have occurred in the absence of its contribution. More important, the bailout turned out to be a temporary measure, and the bank was allowed to fail six months after the attempted rescue. Other Canadian experiences, however, do support O'Driscoll's point. In the early 20th century, several banks that were about to fail merged with sound banks precisely to internalize the costs to depositors of bank failures and hence head off any potential contagion. In 1986 the Mercantile Bank and the National Bank merged for similar reasons.

In the last 10 years, at least five agencies have examined the provision of deposit insurance in Canada; options such as coinsurance and risk-related premiums and alternative limits on insured deposits have been considered. The most recent study (Economic Council of Canada 1987) recommended retaining the status quo, arguing that risk-related premiums would either be backward looking or very costly if they were based on a thorough analysis of an institution's current loan portfolio. That seems to be a weak rationale for rejecting such premiums, since presumably depositors, at least wholesale depositors whose funds are not insured, must undertake such an evaluation before they make a deposit. The Economic Council also rejected the option of coinsurance, arguing that it would provide insufficient protection for small investors.

One change that would not significantly alter the status quo would be the introduction of a deposit redemption fund. Although the CDIC has compensated all insured depositors, it has often done so after several months, so that depositors have lost interest or liquidity, or both. A deposit redemption fund, patterned after the BCRF, would compensate insured depositors immediately and then be reimbursed by the CDIC.

Although the assignment of banks to risk classes that paid different deposit insurance premiums would begin to address the moral hazard problem, there remains a question of whether a government monopoly on deposit insurance is necessary. In Canada the size of the Big 5 banks suggests that only the government could credibly commit to insure their depositors.[21]

## Conclusion

As I suggested at the outset, few general conclusions emerge. It is useful, however, to contrast the role of the Canadian and U.S. governments in payment services. Canadian government intervention lagged behind that of the United States. The Bank of Canada was formed in 1935, two decades after the Fed; the CDIC began business in 1967, more than three decades after the FDIC; the clearing system is still privately operated; private banks issued their own notes until the 1940s—without a provision (such as the U.S. national banks had) that they be 100 percent backed by government bonds.

The concentration of the Canadian banking system goes a long way toward explaining the smaller role of the government. Bank insolvency— particularly since the beginning of the 20th century—has been a rare event; thus there has been less need for deposit insurance. Financial panics are less devastating in a widely branched banking system. That may explain the earlier emergence of the Fed, and also the importance of banking policy relative to monetary policy, in the United States. While there is considerably less supervision of banks in Canada, it is not clear if that reflects less need for supervision or more politically powerful banks. Finally, the advantage of the concentrated nature of the Canadian banking system is that it makes coordination easier, and that may explain why the clearing system has always been privately operated.

## Notes

1. In the former case, the total stock of high-powered money need not change because any loan to an individual bank can be offset by an open-market operation. In the latter case, the goal of the central bank is to increase liquidity and thereby increase the total stock of high-powered money.

2. Trust companies originally focused on trustee activities, but recently an increasing share of their business has been financial intermediation. A majority of their funds are obtained from one- to five-year term deposits and are invested in mortgages. *Caisses populaires* are financial cooperatives that lend only to members.

3. See Shearer, Chant, and Bond (1984) for a discussion of the history of Canadian bank regulation.

4. The Royal Bank held 22 percent of total bank assets; the Canadian Imperial Bank of Commerce, 19 percent; the Bank of Montreal, 16 percent; the Bank of Nova Scotia, 15 percent; and the Toronto Dominion Bank, 12 percent.

5. The supervisory process is described in more detail in Estey (1986).

6. See "Canadian Payments Association By-law" (1983, Sec. 10.01). Anvari (1990) provides a good overview of the operations of the CPA.

7. As of July 1986, "the postings to the accounts of the direct clearers are backdated one business day on the books of the Bank of Canada thus, de facto, there is no clearing float in the system" (Anvari 1988, p. 8).

8. See "Canadian Payments Association By-law" (1983, Sec. 20).

9. See "Canadian Payments Association By-law" (1983 Sec. 20.03c).

10. See "Canadian Payments Association By-law" (1983, Sec. 20.04).

11. The directors of the CPA may suspend membership rights of an institution that does not behave in accordance with the by-laws and rules. (CPA General By-law, Sec. 12). Compare Goodfriend (1988), who argues that historically the threat of expulsion from a clearinghouse provided an important incentive for members of private clearinghouses in the United States.

12. Under an agency agreement the CDIC asks another member institution to administer (that is, wind down) the assets and liabilities of the insolvent member. The CDIC advances or guarantees funds advanced by the agent to meet depositor claims.

13. Depositors with uninsured deposits at trust companies that failed have not been compensated.

14. The Financial Institutions Depositors Compensation Act (S.C. 1985, c. 51).

15. In today's terms between $250 and $1,000, depending on whether purchasing power is measured in units of bread or labor.

16. A decisive movement toward the current oligopolistic structure occurred between 1900 and 1920 when, primarily as a result of mergers, the number of banks fell from 35 to 12.

17. As noted earlier, the distribution is highly skewed; the Big 5 average $82.6 billion, while the other five Schedule A banks average $7.3 billion.

18. Free daylight overdrafts have presumably also increased the use of Fedwire relative to a clearing system without free daylight overdrafts and driven the price of intraday loans close to zero.

19. The need for a lender of last resort during systemwide banking crises is defined by Goodfriend and King (1988) as a need for monetary rather than banking policy. They argue that such policy is necessary, and the events of October 1987, in both Canada and the United States go a long way toward establishing that position.

20. "It is fair to conclude that if competition had reigned in North American banking, Canada would have had many more independent banks" (O'Driscoll 1988, p. 177).

21. That is analogous to the argument that Fedwire-type overdrafts would not be offered by a private clearinghouse.

## References

Anvari, Mohsen. 1990. "The Canadian Payment System: An Evolving Structure." In *The U.S. Payment System: Efficiency, Risk, and the Role of the Federal*

*Reserve*, proceeding of a symposium sponsored by the Federal Reserve Bank of Richmond, May 25–26, 1988, edited by David B. Humphrey, pp. 93–121. Boston: Kluwer Academic Publishers.

Canada, Department of Finance. 1976. "White Paper on the Revision of Canadian Banking Legislation." Ottawa: Ministry of Supply and Services Canada.

Canada, Department of Finance. 1978. "Summary of Banking Legislation." Ottawa: Ministry of Supply and Services Canada.

Canada Deposit Insurance Corporation. Various years. *Annual Report*. Ottawa: CDIC.

Canadian Payments Association. 1988. *Annual Review*. Ottawa: CPA.

"Canadian Payments Association By-law no. 3—Clearing Bylaw." 1983. *Canada Gazette* 117, no. 3 (January 15).

Chant, John. 1987. "Regulation of Financial Institutions—A Functional Analysis." Bank of Canada Technical Report no. 45. Ottawa: Bank of Canada.

Denison, Merrill. 1967. *Canada's First Bank*, vol. 2. Toronto: McClelland and Stewart.

Economic Council of Canada. 1987. "A Framework for Financial Regulation." Ottawa: Ministry of Supply and Services Canada.

Estey, Willard Z. 1986. *Report of the Inquiry into the Collapse of the CCB and Northland Bank*. Ottawa: Ministry of Supply and Services Canada.

Goodfriend, Marvin. 1988. "Money, Credit, Banking and Payments System Policy." Federal Reserve Bank of Richmond, Virginia. Unpublished manuscript.

Goodfriend, Marvin, and King, Robert G. 1988. "Financial Deregulation, Monetary Policy and Central Banking." Federal Reserve Bank of Richmond *Economic Review* 74 (May/June): 3–22.

Gorton, G. 1985. "Clearinghouses and the Origin of Central Banking in the U.S." *Journal of Economic History* 45, pp. 277–83.

Humphrey, David Burras. 1986. "Payments Finality and Risk of Settlement Failure." In *Technology and Regulation of Financial Markets*, edited by Anthony Saunders and Lawrence J. White. Lexington, Mass.: Lexington Books, pp. 97–120.

McIvor, R. Craig. 1961. *Canadian Monetary Banking and Fiscal Development*. Toronto: Macmillan.

Martin, Peter. 1985. *Inside the Bank of Canada's Weekly Financial Statistics: A Technical Guide*. Vancouver: Fraser Institute.

O'Driscoll, Gerald P., Jr. 1988. "Deposit Insurance in Theory and Practice." In *The Financial Services Revolution*, edited by Catherine England and Thomas Huertas, pp. 165–79. Washington D.C.: Cato Institute.

Shearer, R. A., Chant, J. F., and Bond, D. E. 1984. *The Economics of the Canadian Financial System*. Scarborough, Ontario: Prentice-Hall.

Smith, Adam. [1776] 1978. *The Wealth of Nations*. Reprint. Toronto: Penguin Books.

Vachon, Serge. 1987. "Evolution 1987." *Bank of Canada Review* (October): 9–14.

# COMMENT ON PAYMENT SYSTEM RISK

## Mark J. Flannery

Each of the papers by Clair, Milano, and Redish offers a different perspective on payment systems, and each concentrates on a different aspect of the issue. After reading all three, I decided I could contribute the most by addressing a question that cuts across all the papers: Why is banking's future closely related to what appears to be the arcane, operational issue of payment system risk? Put another way, why is more than 30 percent of this book devoted to papers about the payment system, when the broader issue under discussion is whether the market or regulators should govern banking's future? My comments address two major questions:

1. Why do we care about payment system risk?
2. What actions are appropriate for controlling that risk?

As Clair and Milano point out, payment system risk issues for a provisional payment system such as the Clearing House Interbank Payment

---

The author is Barnett Banks Professor of Finance at the University of Florida.

System (CHIPS) differ qualitatively from the issues related to Fedwire. The two systems' policy and managerial issues must therefore be addressed separately. I will begin with CHIPS and then turn to the issues associated with daylight overdrafts on Fedwire. Finally, I will discuss the best means of solving either or both sets of supposed problems.

## Why Do We Care?

### CHIPS

Security on the provisional payment CHIPS system raises regulatory and managerial concerns, both of which derive from the same basic issue: whether credit risks are being properly monitored. The Fed—and within the Fed most notably E. Gerald Corrigan, president of the Federal Reserve Bank of New York—has been extremely concerned that a single bank's failure to settle on CHIPS could have detrimental effects not only for that bank but also for other CHIPS participants. That possibility is called systemic risk or, more ominously, a "financial system meltdown." I fully concur that we should avoid a meltdown, but I have never completely understood the mechanism by which such a meltdown would occur, especially if each member of CHIPS prudently diversifies its own intraday credit exposure.

Nevertheless, the possibility that a CHIPS settlement failure might become systemic has engendered two major Fed actions:

1. In exchange for same-day settlement through the New York Fed, CHIPS was required to develop a system of bilateral daylight caps. (Both Clair and Milano point out that the rigor with which those caps are applied by CHIPS exceeds the Fed's ability to control daylight overdrafts on its own wire system.)
2. The Fed has opposed bank mergers with nonbanking firms because, according to the Fed, such alliances might increase the likelihood of initial bank settlement failures.

In short, payment system risk is important for two reasons: because of the meltdown possibility and because the Fed has introduced meaningful regulations to supplement private controls to protect against that possibility.

## *Fedwire*

Clair clearly explains that Fedwire involves no systemic risk because the Fed explicitly guarantees all payments. The problem here is that unpriced daylight credit generates inefficiencies in a market-based system. The Fed's willingness to bear daylight credit risk for free distorts incentives to private market participants. In particular, banks will not monitor the risk of their counterparties in Fedwire transactions, and they will collectively underinvest in mechanisms for avoiding and monitoring daylight credits. While society gains an effortlessly reliable transaction system, taxpayers must bear risks that they are in no position to control.

The regulatory and managerial concerns associated with Fedwire are less coincident than are those associated with CHIPS. The regulatory issue is whether intraday credit losses should be borne by the Fed. More to the point (as Clair emphasizes), should taxpayers bear the intraday credit risk? That question has both an efficiency and an equity dimension, and I am unaware of any formal effort to compare the associated costs and benefits of Fedwire finality. Does the public's benefit from a reliable payment mechanism outweigh the costs of daylight overdrafts that result from attaining reliability via Fedwire payment finality? Such an assessment would be extremely difficult to undertake, but it crucially affects our view of daylight overdrafts on Fedwire.

Fedwire's provision of free intraday credit also raises two managerial issues. First, any substantial change in the current overdraft policy will require compensating adjustments by bankers, undoubtedly at some expense. (Expenses would include investment in additional technology and perhaps additional credit risk associated with banks' daily business.) The efficiency question is whether existing payment and risk-bearing arrangements are the least-cost means of making payments across large geographic distances.

Second, a small number of banks view the Fed as an important—and unfair—competitor in the payment business. As Kane (1982) has pointed out, there is simply no way a private payment processor can ensure the same level of finality the Fed can. And if the Fed does not charge for that finality, private processors cannot compete very successfully. Would-be competitors reason that if the Fed were to price its Fedwire services fully (as apparently is required by the Monetary Control Act of 1980), private payment networks would achieve a greater market share, and hence greater profits. (Of course, the new entrants' transaction service customers would also gain.)

## What Should We Do?

*CHIPS*

The obvious response to systemic risk on CHIPS is for managers and supervisors to ensure that daylight risks are prudently monitored and controlled. The fact that a credit is scheduled to disappear before sunset does not make it less a credit. If individual banks are not exposed to excessive risk by other participants, a CHIPS failure may induce illiquidity—especially because the settlement failure occurs when short-term financial markets are effectively closed for the day—but it will not render other banks insolvent. As a result, the lender of last resort has both the duty and the opportunity to provide liquidity to CHIPS participants that have monitored their individual credit exposures properly.

The only difference I see between that type of credit risk and the more usual situation is the intensity with which problems can hit. A late-in-the-day settlement failure puts immense pressure on the New York Federal Reserve Bank to make an important, highly visible solvency assessment. Though that sounds ominous, recall that banks do not generally go broke quickly. Consequently, the Fed should already have been monitoring the banks that are most likely to be rendered insolvent by a settlement failure. If we cannot rely on the lender of last resort in such a situation, I wonder when we can rely on it.

But suppose the Fed cannot make those important solvency judgments in a reliably accurate fashion. Then fear of an impending meltdown would lead the Fed to lend generously to any illiquid CHIPS bank, regardless of its true condition. Under that scenario, the federal safety net would provide de facto 100 percent liability insurance, and we would have efficiency and incentive problems that would be far more extensive than are those generated by CHIPS payment system risk.

What about the Fed's two regulatory responses to CHIPS default risks? The system of bilateral caps is a reasonable and prudent management tool, especially since individual banks are free to limit their own exposure to each CHIPS counterparty. In that instance, it appears that the Fed has helped bankers to recognize a connection between operational issues and credit issues that previously did not receive sufficient managerial attention. In contrast, I fail to see why a merger of banking and commerce is per se dangerous to payment system stability. Such combinations may or may not be a good idea, but their value has little to do with payment system risk. Rather, we must evaluate such mergers in terms of the issues discussed in earlier sections of this book—in particular, the effectiveness of Federal Reserve Act Section 23A and 23B restrictions on interaffiliate transactions.

## Fedwire

We can solve the problem of unpriced daylight overdrafts on Fedwire either by *eliminating* them or by *pricing* them. At first glance, it seems most reasonable to permit no Fedwire overdrafts at all. Redish reports that that is the basic system employed by the Bank of Canada, and it is surely the system applied to my own checking account.

With existing Fedwire technology, the Fed continuously monitors the reserve accounts of only a small number of banks. Such monitoring involves a fairly complex coordination of the wire transfer system with the collection systems for checks, food stamps, Treasury coupons, and the like. It is important to recognize that the problem is primarily *operational*; it demands a careful cost-benefit analysis. The cost of monitoring more banks may exceed the marginal benefits. If so, one wonders how large that dimension of the payment system risk problem really is.

Because the Fed is currently unable to monitor reserve balances continuously, it has three policy alternatives:

1. Do not monitor reserve balances continuously and impose loose caps. Essentially, maintain the status quo.
2. Do not monitor reserve balances continuously, but price overdrafts ex post.
3. Invest in the technology needed to monitor reserves continuously and forbid overdrafts, or price them, or cap them.

Clair indicates that the existing caps have not significantly reduced over-drafts. Further tightening the caps might have the desired effect, but the problem with quantity constraints alone is that there is no means of pricing the constraint, and thus no means of assessing its efficiency. On the other hand, controlling private activities through administered prices will not work perfectly either, because the task of setting a correct price on credit is very difficult.

Administered caps or prices that do not accurately reflect risk will create distortions—but then, so does the present system. The magnitude of any new distortions depends crucially on the availability of close substitutes for traditional ways of effecting payments. If existing payment arrangements have evolved because they are intrinsically more efficient than alternatives, then we should worry about the accuracy of Fed pricing.

However, I believe that existing institutional arrangements have evolved primarily because the Fed's policies largely eliminated any reason to develop alternative arrangements. If that is the case, substitute transaction methods may be readily available and almost equally efficient. The evidence indicates that changing several key institutional features would most probably eliminate the daylight overdraft problem. In particular:

1. substituting term federal funds and repurchase agreements for one-day transactions,
2. further liberalizing conventions about partial securities market deliveries, and
3. introducing netting procedures for bilateral flows of funds.

Though our existing payment arrangements did not create serious problems in the past, recent developments have increased the flow of payments relative to average reserve balances. It is now advisable to alter traditional payment practices. Because other arrangements can reduce daylight overdrafts and still substitute closely for current practices, any increase in the explicit or implicit cost of daylight overdrafts on Fedwire would probably generate a desirable response. The important change is from today's effective cost of zero to some (indeed, to any) positive cost. We could then observe whether private-sector solutions of the types listed above can easily resolve the problem.

Should the Fed install the expensive technological capacity required to eliminate daylight overdrafts entirely? I would argue against that option for the present because I expect alternative payment arrangements will emerge quickly. If continuous monitoring seems advisable sometime in the future, we can probably limit it to the largest banks, which run the vast bulk of all daylight overdrafts. Until we know that the problem cannot be easily fixed, however, it is not worthwhile to incur drastic new expenses.

## Summary

The issue of payment system risk is not central to the future of banking. Though the scale of credit extensions indicated by Clair's and Milano's numbers cannot be dismissed out of hand, daylight overdraft risk is but one manifestation of the credit risk banks regularly encounter. For that reason, CHIPS participants must monitor intraday credit prudently if they are to operate in a safe and sound fashion. If they do not, the regulator has adequate grounds for concern and adequate cause for action under existing statutes and regulatory procedures.

On Fedwire, several modest policy changes probably would substantially reduce the use of intraday credit. As the first step toward rationalizing payment system procedures, the important thing is to get away from completely free daylight overdrafts and impose some positive price. Fedwire payment system risk must be viewed largely as an issue of operational efficiency, and it should not be permitted to influence other, already complex considerations about the proper structure and role of banking firms in the economy.

## Reference

Kane, Edward J. 1982. "Changes in the Provision of Correspondent Banking Services and the Role of Federal Reserve Banks under the DIDMC Act." *Carnegie-Rochester Conference Series on Public Policy* 16, pp. 93–126.

# 10 A PROPOSAL TO RELY ON MARKET INTEREST RATES ON INTRADAY FUNDS TO REDUCE PAYMENT SYSTEM RISK

Wayne D. Angell

The appropriate balance between market-based and regulatory solutions is a problem with which the Federal Reserve has struggled, particularly during the past decade as the economy and payment system have become more global. Until now the Fed has focused primarily on regulatory solutions. I would like to outline the reasons for the struggle and compare a regulatory approach with a market-determined solution. I would also like to spend a little time discussing the use of the U.S. dollar as the key currency in the international payment mechanism and the lack of a meaningful intraday funds market. Before I start, however, I want to describe a trap that we in the public sector frequently fall into when addressing complex issues.

Society is faced with many complex issues that government agencies, both on the local and the national level, must face each day. Typically, the first thing we do is assign the problem to technical experts, who are asked to develop alternative solutions. Using their expertise, the technicians often develop very complex solutions that, by their very nature, have a regulatory bent.

The author is a member of the Board of Governors of the Federal Reserve System.

Consider the administration of farm subsidies, for example. The administered subsidies frequently encourage farmers to plant crops for which there is no marketplace demand, thereby allocating resources inefficiently. Oats, for example, have been in high demand in the United States in recent months because of the increased public awareness of the health benefits of oat bran. Yet the farm program has had the effect of inducing farmers to grow more corn and wheat and less oats. As a result, the United States has become a net importer of oats, although it was once a net exporter. That example illustrates in a concrete way how regulatory solutions often bring about market inefficiencies.

## The Nature of the Problem

The Federal Reserve has been concerned for some time about the risk associated with large-dollar payment systems, including the Federal Reserve's Fedwire service and the private Clearing House Interbank Payment System (CHIPS). When the Federal Reserve receives instructions from a bank that has an account with it to transfer funds to another bank, the Federal Reserve generally effects the transfer and sends the receiver an advice of the transfer. Because the Federal Reserve treats the payment to the receiving bank as an irrevocable payment, it is exposed to the risk of loss if the bank sending the payment does not have sufficient funds in its account to cover the payment. Likewise, when a bank sends a government security to another bank through Fedwire, the Federal Reserve gives irrevocable credit to the sending bank for the purchase price of the security. If the bank receiving the security does not have sufficient funds in its reserve account to pay for the security, a daylight overdraft is created, and the Federal Reserve has given away free reserve bank credit.

Currently, the Federal Reserve's daily aggregate credit exposure averages $115 billion: $55 billion in intraday Fedwire funds transfer overdrafts and $60 billion in book-entry securities transfer overdrafts.

Participants in the private CHIPS network are exposed to two types of risk—individual credit risk and systemic risk. Transfers among CHIPS participants are provisional until the net balances of the participants are settled on the books of the Federal Reserve at the close of business. Because payments are provisional, institutions that permit their customers to use those funds are exposed to the individual credit risk that one or more CHIPS participants will be unable to settle their net debit positions at the close of business and that their customers will not be able to repay the provisional funds to which they were given access during the day.

CHIPS participants are also exposed to systemic risk. If one participant cannot settle its net debit position at the close of business, the network, under the CHIPS rules, must unwind worldwide the day's payment transactions that involve the illiquid depository institution. Simulations of that process indicate that participants' positions can change dramatically. Institutions originally in net credit positions can become net debtors, and those already in net debit positions may experience significant increases in their net debit positions. More important, the simulations show that the failure of one medium-sized CHIPS participant to settle could lead to the failure to settle of nearly one-half of the other participants.

## Current Risk Policy

To prevent the Federal Reserve from shielding participants from those credit risks and to reduce the systemic risk of private large-dollar funds transfer networks, the Federal Reserve instituted a Payment System Risk Reduction Program in the late 1970s. Thus far, the program has had a regulatory orientation, establishing credit limits for Fedwire and CHIPS participants. The intraday credit limits, which we call daylight overdraft caps, are expressed as multiples of depository institutions' capital. Depository institutions that incur daylight overdrafts on Fedwire or that participate on CHIPS must perform a self-evaluation of their creditworthiness and their operational control and credit policies, which is later verified through financial examination. Institutions with high ratings are permitted to select larger caps than are those with lower ratings. The managers of institutions whose overdrafts exceed their predetermined caps are counseled by the Federal Reserve. The CHIPS network has also instituted bilateral credit limits to establish the credit exposure each participant will accept from every other participant. Through the use of overdraft caps, the Federal Reserve has put boundaries around its aggregate credit exposure, but the Fed has not done enough to reduce the systemic risk faced by CHIPS and other private networks.

The regulatory approach has controlled Federal Reserve risk. The Federal Reserve's aggregate intraday credit exposure has been reduced from more than 10 cents per dollar transferred, when the policy was introduced, to less than 8 cents per dollar now. In addition, the number of institutions incurring daylight overdrafts declined from 3,600 in 1985 to around 2,200 in 1988. Despite those achievements, there is no assurance that daylight credit is being allocated efficiently.

During 1988 the Federal Reserve took an entirely fresh look at the adequacy of its program to control payment system risk. We concluded that a long-run strategy to control risk will require the careful balancing of the risk borne by the Federal Reserve against that borne by the private sector.

In crafting a future policy to control risk, the Federal Reserve needs to consider carefully the tradeoffs associated with a regulatory solution versus those arising under a market-oriented approach. We do not want the risk abatement program to slow payment flows, to increase the cost of transmitting payments unduly, or to drive payments to a nonfinal clearinghouse arrangement. We must also be sensitive to the possibility of driving payments offshore as well as the program's competitive impact on providers of payment services. Moreover, we must be aware that our daylight overdraft policy interrelates with the conduct of monetary policy and may affect the market for Treasury securities.

The available administered policy options are well known. We can, for example,

1. lower caps,
2. adopt explicit prices on intraday credit extensions,
3. require collateral to cover daylight overdrafts,
4. impose higher clearing balances, or
5. adopt a combination of those policy steps.

There is considerable sentiment for an administrative solution, such as the Federal Reserve's setting a fee to be applied to intraday overdrafts. Imposing explicit prices for intraday credit would provide monetary incentives for depository institutions to avoid overdrafts by adopting more efficient payment practices, such as netting. Unfortunately, there are fundamental problems inherent in such administrative solutions. It could be difficult to determine the appropriate policy structure to "mimic" market efficiency. The inflexibility of policy responses to changing market conditions could also be a major shortcoming. There is, in addition, the moral hazard problem that could arise in an administered environment. If private markets for intraday credit did develop under an administered system, private market rates would not rise above administered rates. Private institutions could not effectively ration credit at the administered rate when confronted with poor credit risks; poor risks would presumably turn to the Federal Reserve for credit. When credit risk is not priced, it is not rationed, and societal risk is not minimized. In other words, administered prices—whether they are price floors or ceiling prices—cannot be expected to work differently for intraday credit than for the oil or housing markets.

## A Market-Based Solution

I have been developing an alternative approach that avoids the problems associated with an administered solution and that should enable the market to allocate intraday credit efficiently. If and when the Fed no longer supplied intraday credit "free of charge," intraday interest rates would reflect the following four factors: (1) transaction costs, (2) pure interest, (3) a credit risk premium, and (4) time-of-day variations in demand. The time-of-day factor would take account of intraday patterns in the use of credit, given a somewhat inelastic supply. Thus, the intraday rate would tend to peak in the afternoon during periods of strong demand and would be lowest in the morning hours when demand is generally lowest.

There are four key elements to my proposal. First, intraday overdrafts at the reserve banks would be automatically swept into collateralized discount window borrowing. Unsecured borrowings or overdrafts would have to be covered within minutes after they occurred, rather than wait until final settlement at the end of the day. Second, although standard collateral would be required for Federal Reserve credit, the discount window would be open to all qualifying institutions as a 24-hour source of money. Since the discount window would be open, depository institutions would not be willing to pay a federal funds rate that was above the discount rate. Third, an overnight (15-hour) rate, which would normally be below the 24-hour market interest rate on funds, would be paid on excess reserve holdings of banks. The present reserve requirement system is in effect only during the 15-hour business day. Fourth, the Federal Reserve's Fedwire network would operate 24 hours a day.

My proposal offers several advantages. The Federal Reserve would no longer be a direct supplier of intraday credit at zero or other subsidized rates. It would, instead, foster the formation of a private market in intraday funds in which the price of such funds would be determined competitively by the forces of supply and demand. Funds would be traded at a market-determined intraday rate of interest that would fully reflect intraday variances in demand and the opportunity costs of the 24-hour alternate rate as well as the marginal cost of increased turnover and the risk premiums that would vary among market participants. Another advantage is that current administrative restraints on discount window borrowing would be replaced by the disincentive of a variable interest rate.

One of the most important features of the proposal is that banks would have an incentive to expand their holdings of excess reserves, especially in light of the variable penalty associated with overdrawing their accounts. The interest earned on those excess reserves would partially offset the opportunity cost of retaining idle funds overnight. However, the banks would still incur some opportunity cost associated with the excess reserves, because the interest rate paid by the Fed would be below the market rate on 24-hour funds. That element of the proposal also produces a policy-determined floor under the 24-hour funds rate. Finally, my proposal would help to avoid the moral hazard issue I mentioned earlier. Specifically, any poor credit risks rationed out of the private intraday market would be forced to borrow from the Federal Reserve at a penalty and to provide acceptable collateral for the amounts of their loans.

Under the market price approach, the public sector's role in supplying intraday credit would be minimized. The competitive forces of supply and demand for intraday credit should result in a more efficient allocation of credit without the Federal Reserve's playing a major role as the provider of intraday funds. It should also reduce total risk by providing a price motivation to improve balance sheets and to avoid clearing arrangements with high systemic risk.

Although it is theoretically possible to use caps to achieve the same allocation of daylight credit that would be obtained in a competitive environment, it would be difficult, if not impossible, for the Federal Reserve to determine the appropriate degree of restraint on credit use.

Caps or other administrative approaches also fail to deal with moral hazard, and fail to provide the incentives to accomplish intraday finality. If caps are set too low, banks and their customers are constrained to a volume of daylight credit that is too low from the perspective of optimizing social welfare. Furthermore, supply and demand conditions change over time, but caps are set at fixed values during short or intermediate periods. Thus, even if the caps established by the Federal Reserve are appropriate when they are set, variations in the demand for intraday credit will cause the socially optimal quantity of credit to diverge from the ceiling quantity imposed by the caps, resulting in departures from economic efficiency.

## Transfer Networks

Now let me turn to the international dimension of large-dollar transfer networks. The dollar is the reserve currency of the world and the currency of choice for many international payments. With the globalization of financial markets, international money movements have become a 24-hour reality. Yet the U.S. large-dollar payment system operates within the U.S. business day. There is no way to make a dollar payment with the certainty of a Fedwire transfer except between 9:00 a.m. and 6:30 p.m. eastern time.

For that reason, banks use other mechanisms, such as privately operated networks along the lines of that operating in Tokyo, to exchange dollar payments. The transfers made over those networks are ultimately settled when CHIPS participants settle with the Federal Reserve at the end of the following business day. That means that a receiver of a transfer may have to wait as long as 20 hours to determine whether the payment has been finally settled. That settlement delay could be reduced substantially if the Federal Reserve funds transfer network operated 24 hours a day.

Other countries with hard currencies, such as Switzerland, already successfully operate funds transfer systems 24 hours a day. In practice, probably only U.S. banks with significant operations in foreign markets and large foreign-based multinational banks would participate in a 24-hour Fedwire System. I would also expect that international transfers would be conveyed to the 24-hour Fedwire via a private international network.

The participating banks would each maintain a special clearing account. Balances in their special clearing accounts would not be counted toward the banks' reserve requirements, and the accounts would be restricted to funds transfers. The balances in the special accounts would not receive interest, even if the Federal Reserve decided to pay interest on clearing account balances in the future. The participants would be free to send and receive transfers using their accounts 24 hours a day, but they would not be able to overdraw their special accounts at any time. At the opening of business, each bank could transfer funds from its special account to its regular reserve or clearing account.

The primary benefit of the 24-hour service would be to provide banks the opportunity to make final payments 24 hours a day, thereby reducing temporal risk. It would also help to ensure that international financial markets continue to operate smoothly around the clock.

Twenty-four-hour Fedwire operation and a market-determined solution to the problem of payment system risk could work hand in hand to reduce payment system risk worldwide. Most important, however, I believe the needed changes can be achieved within the next few years through the normal interactions of market forces. By allowing the market to operate freely within a limited number of rules and by providing an operational mechanism to facilitate the international settlement of large-dollar payments, the Federal Reserve can take a large step toward controlling risk while promoting market efficiency.

In summary, I support a market-based approach to addressing the credit risk arising from the operation of large-dollar funds transfer networks that avoids the problems associated with the present system and some proposed administered solutions.

# Index

Accountability, political, 83
Agricultural Adjustment Act (1933)
  Thomas Amendment (Title III), 100
Anvari, Mohsen, 168
Association of Reserve City Bankers, 138n1

Bailouts, 70, 81–85, 88–89, 93, 99, 171,
    176–77
  cost of, 98–99
  of nonbank subsidiaries, 66
  safety net as program for, 73
Bank Acts, Canada, 164, 170
Bank Circulation Redemption Fund
    (BCRF), Canada, 170, 177
Bank failures
  effect on deposit insurance system of,
    95–96
  increase in number of, 3–4
  See also Safety net provisions
Bank Holding Company Act, 63–64
Banking institutions
  competition from nonbank institutions,
    4–5
  differentiation from nonbanking
    institutions, 71–72
  future requirements for, 70–72
  redefinition of, 73–75
Banking institutions, international
  common capital standards for, 24
  U.S.-Canadian standards for, 28

Banking system
  effect of regulation differences on, 67–70
  proposed reforms for U.S., 16
  requirement for interstate banking policy
    for, 16
  response to G-10 capital agreement of
    U.S., 40–41
  risk in, 4
  source-of-strength policy for, 5, 13, 64
  See also Depository institutions
Banking system, Canada
  concentration of, 178
  development of, 162–65
  regulation of, 172–75
  See also Bank of Canada, Canadian
    Payments Association (CPA)
Banking system, dual, 51–52, 53
Banking system, EC, 42
Bank insulation
  current status and feasibility of, 12–13,
    60–61, 112–13
  efficacy of, 66–67, 112–13
  Federal Reserve Board position on,
    62–66
  issue of, 59–60, 64
  law weakening, 61
  from nonbank affiliates, 54, 62–66,
    72–75
  proposals to improve, 61–62
  purpose of, 62
  reasons for, 12

197

role of Federal Reserve in, 75
safety net role in, 94–98, 112
*See also* Safety net provisions
Bank Insurance Fund, 100
Bank of Canada, 163, 167–69
as lender of last resort, 169, 174–76
note issue policy of, 171–72
risk exposure of, 175
Bank rescues. *See* Bailouts
Basle capital agreement, 6, 15, 21, 24–26, 34–35, 38–42
*See also* Capital; Capital system; Group of 10; Regulation, bank
Baumol, William, 36
BCRF. *See* Bank Circulation Redemption Fund (BCRF)
Belton, Terrence M., 127
Bennett, Barbara A., 75
Bond, D. E., 172

Caliguire, Daria B., 86, 102n23
Canada, Department of Finance, 166
Canada Deposit Insurance Corporation (CDIC), 169–71, 174–75, 177–78
Canadian Bankers' Association (CBA), 165
Canadian Commercial Bank (CCB), 171, 176–77
Canadian Payments Association (CPA), 166–69
Cannon, James G., 159n7
Capital, eligible, 38–39
Capital system, international
effect of risk-based agreement for, 34–35, 38–42
risk-based standards for, 15–16, 21, 24–26, 29, 52–53
*See also* Cartel, Regulation, bank
Cartel: defined, 39–40
formation of by agreement, 6
private and regulatory, 34–35
CBA. *See* Canadian Bankers' Association (CBA)
CDIC. *See* Canada Deposit Insurance Corporation (CDIC)
Central bank. *See also* Bank of Canada, Federal Reserve System
Central bank role, 22, 25, 35–36, 83, 90–94, 100–1, 112

Chant, J. F., 172, 173
Chase, Laub & Company, 31n3, 31n4, 60, 76n8, 107
CHIPS. *See* Clearing House Interbank Payment System (CHIPS), New York Clearing House Association
Clair, Robert T., 123, 142, 159n10
Clearing House Interbank Payment System (CHIPS), 119–23
credit policy of, 151–53, 159n15
effect of risk reduction policies on, 125–31
effect of settlement failure risk in, 132, 182
proposal to lower credit risk of, 184
*See also* Payment systems, international
Clearing houses. *See* Canadian Bankers' Association, Canadian Payments Association (CPA), Clearing House Interbank Payment System, Fedwire Payment system, Payment systems
Competitive Equality Banking Act (1987), 61
Cooper, Kerry, 76n1
Corporate separateness principle, 29, 54, 64
*See also* Bank insulation
Corrigan, E. Gerald, 152
Cox, Edwin, 76n1
CPA. *See* Canadian Payments Association (CPA)
Credit allocation, 84
Credit risk: Federal Reserve System policy for, 135–36, 137, 148–53
pricing policy for, 153–58
proposal for market-based solution for, 193–95
Credit transfer systems, 146–48

Deficit financing, 90–94
Denison, Merrill, 165
Deposit insurance law, 85–90
Deposit insurance system
effect of bank failures on, 95–96
effect of credit risk policy on, 154–55
effect of Treasury lending to, 92–93
with international cooperation, 52
limits for, 100
trend to expand, 88–90

*See also* Federal Deposit Insurance
    Corporation (FDIC), Federal Savings
    and Loan Insurance Corporation
    (FSLIC)
Deposit insurance system, Canada, 176–78
Depository institutions
    perspectives on risk-taking of, 94–98
    subsidizing activities of, 82–83
    terms used in discussion of, 81–82
    *See also* Deposit insurance system
Depository Institutions Deregulation and
    Monetary Control Act (1980), 8n1,
    152, 183
Dewey, Davis R., 101n6
Diamond, Douglas, 55n1
Double-umbrella concept. *See* Holding
    companies, bank, Holding companies,
    financial services or nonbank
Duffy, John J., 42
Duke, Paul, Jr., 97
Dybvig, Philip H., 55n1


Economic Council of Canada, 177
Ely, Bert, 95–96, 103n33
Estey, Willard Z., 173–74
European Community (EC), 15–16
    effect of regulation of financial markets
        by, 34–35
    integration of financial institutions of,
        15–16, 21, 26–28, 42–44
European Council, 42


Federal Deposit Insurance Corporation
    (FDIC)
    changing fiat and effect of, 85–90
    credit risk responsibility of, 154–55
    as lender of last resort, 82
    liquidity and capital sources for, 83
    using double-umbrella concept, 14
    *See also* Bank Insurance Fund, Deposit
        insurance system
Federal Reserve Act
    amendments affecting bank insulation of,
        61
    purchase of Treasury obligations under,
        92

Sections 23A&B, bank insulation under,
    60–61, 63, 65
Federal Reserve System
    assistance to banks and FDIC by, 92–94,
        112
    Board of Governors, 102n29
    credit transfer policy of, 147–48
    Electronic Clearing House Study (1988),
        141
    Fedwire payment system of, 119–23
    intraday credit policy of, 135–36, 137,
        148–53, 183, 191–92
    as lender of last resort, 95, 112
    position on bank insulation of, 62–66,
        107–8
    price mechanism for daylight overdrafts,
        7
    proposed policy for payment system risk
        of, 134–37
    regulation of payment systems by,
        125–31
    role in insulation of, 75
    *See also* Fedwire payment system
    U.S. Department of the Treasury
Federal Savings and Loan Insurance
    Corporation (FSLIC)
    as lender of last resort, 82
    sources of liquidity and capital for, 83
    use of deposit insurance by, 89–90
    *See also* Resolution Trust Corporation
        (RTC), Savings Association Insurance
        Fund
Fedwire payment system, 97, 119–23
    effect of risk reduction policies on,
        126–31, 183
    effect of settlement failure risk in,
        131–32, 183
    intraday credit policy of, 183, 185–87
    proposal to change credit risk policy of,
        185–87
    risk procedure for, 120–21, 175
    *See also* Deposit insurance system
Financial Institutions Reform, Recovery,
    and Enforcement Act (FIRREA),
    1989, 98–101
Financial services industry
    changes and restructuring of, 14–15,
        22–24
    competition in regulation of, 35–38

international interdependence of, 5
proposals to integrate European, 42–44
regulatory markets of, 35–38
*See also* Holding companies, financial
services or nonbank
Financial services industry
nonbank competitive activity of, 52–53
effect of risk-based capital standards on,
26
FIRREA. *See* Financial Institutions
Reform, Recovery and Enforcement
Act (FIRREA), 1989
Fraser, Donald, 76n1
Friedman, Milton, 94
Friesen, Connie M., 46n2
Furlong, Frederick T., 53

Garn-St Germain Act (1982), 61
Giddy, Ian H., 36
Gilbert, R. Alton, 14
Glass-Steagall Act, 71–72, 108–9, 113
Goodfriend, Marvin, 161, 174, 175, 179n11
Gorton, Gary, 50, 158–59n6, 159n7, 175
Group of 10 (G-10), 6, 15, 17n, 24–26,
38–42

Hamilton, Alexander, 101n6, 102n27
Hammond, Bray, 101n5
Hayek, Friedrich, 101n9
Heinemann, H. Erich, 102n25
Holding companies, bank
activities and operation of, 62–66, 70, 97
double-umbrella concept for, 13–14
effect of bank insulation on, 66–67,
107–8
regulation of, 62–64, 107–110
as source of strength, 64
*See also* Bank Holding Company Act
Holding companies, financial services or
nonbank, 13–14
Holland, Kelley, 102n29
Hollis, Donald R., 159n18
Huhne, Christopher, 102n24
Humphrey, David B., 118, 122, 130, 138n1,
168

Intraday credit. *See* Federal Reserve
System, Payment systems, Price
mechanism

Jefferson, Thomas, 84–85
Jones, Jesse H., 101n7

Kane, Edward J., 34, 44, 45, 46n1, 102n15,
112, 183
Kareken, John, 109, 113
Kaufman, George G., 50
Keeley, Michael C., 53, 75
King, Robert G., 161, 174, 175
Knight, Jerry, 3
Kutler, Jeffrey, 159n14

Lamke, Edwin, 101n7
Lender of first resort (LFR), 84
Lender of last resort (LLR), 113–14
Canadian system of, 169, 174, 175–76
defined, 82
deposit insurance system as, 157
fiat under FIRREA of, 99–100
proposals for activity and responsibility
of, 83–85
role of, 83–85, 113–14
*See also* Bailouts, Federal Reserve
System, Liquidity support, Solvency
support
Lever, Harold, 102n24
LFR. *See* Lender of first resort (LFR)
License, banking, 26–27
Liquidity support, or assistance, 81–85,
99–100
Litan, Robert, 74, 76n1, 103n32
LLR. *See* Lender of last resort (LLR)

McIvor, R. Craig, 170
McTague, Jim, 102n17
Martin, Peter, 169
Mengle, David L., 120, 132, 138n1
Miller, Merton H., 52
Modigliani, Franco, 52
Morgan Guaranty Trust, 42

*Newsweek*, 3
New York Clearing House Association,
    119–23, 138n10
Niskanen, William, 37
Nonbank affiliates. *See* Bank insulation,
    Financial services industry, nonbank,
    Holding companies, bank, Safety net
    provisions

O'Driscoll, Gerald P., Jr., 113, 175,
    176–77, 179n20
Overdrafts, daylight. *See* Clearing House
    Interbank Payment System (CHIPS),
    Federal Reserve System, Fedwire
    payment system, Payment systems

Panzar, John C., 36
Payment system, Canada evolution of,
    162–65; role of government in, 171–78
Payment System Risk Reduction Program,
    191–92
Payment systems
    activities and size of, 141–45
    effect of risk on policy for, 123–25, 182
    existing, 118–25
    finality in credit risk policy, 147–48,
        154–55, 175, 190
    intraday credit activity of, 118, 120–31,
        148–53
    intraday credit risk proposals for, 155–58
    mechanisms for, 145–48
    private, 151–53
    proposals for reform of, 134–37
    risk in current, 7, 117–18, 120–23,
        131–34, 137
    risk reduction policy for, 125–31
    settlement process for, 121–23, 125–34,
        137, 146–48
    *See also* Clearing House Interbank
        Payment System (CHIPS), Fedwire
        payment system, Payment systems,
        international
Payment systems, international, 119,
    194–95
Pearce, David W., 39–40
Peers, Alexandra, 112
Penning, Ann Cooper, 101n7

Perfectly contestable market, 36
Pierce, James L., 7, 10, 12, 76n1
Price mechanism: for intraday credit, 7,
    134–38, 153–54
    in regulatory market structure, 36

Reciprocity policy, non-EC banks, 27–28,
    43
Reconstruction Finance Corporation (RFC)
    as lender of last resort, 82–83
    organization and activity of, 88, 100
Regulation, bank
    alternate proposal for international, 21,
        23–24, 26, 29–30
    attempts to coordinate international,
        15–16, 21, 24–28
    in Canadian banking system, 163–64
    outdated nature of, 4
    proposed framework for international,
        21, 29–30
    purpose of, 22, 50–52, 62
    *See also* Capital system, international;
        European Community (EC) Securities
        market, European Community
Regulation, financial, 33–38
Rehm, Barbara, 102n17
Resolution Trust Corporation (RTC), 100

Safety net, federal
    bank access to, 13–14, 71–75
    extent and role of, 4, 72–75, 81–98, 112
    for nonbank affiliates, 65–66
    protection of bank depositors by,
        12–13
    relationship of banking system to, 6,
        94–98, 112
    *See also* Bailouts, Bank insulation,
        Lender of last resort (LLR)
Safety net provisions, international, 25
Samuel Chase and Company, 31n3
Savings Association Insurance Fund, 100
Schumpeter, Joseph A., 101n9
Scott, Kenneth E., 34
Securities market, European Community,
    42
Settlement failure. *See* Clearing House
    Interbank Payment System (CHIPS),
    Fedwire payment system, Payment
    systems

Shearer, R. A., 172
Smith, Adam, 171–72
Solvency support, 81–82, 88
Source-of-strength policy. *See* Banking system
Spero, Joan E., 102n18
Sprague, Irvine, 102n19
Stigler, George J., 34

Task Force on Controlling Payment System Risk, 4, 138n1, 139n18
Third World country loans, 25
Thomson, James B., 86, 102n23
Todd, Walker F., 82, 101n4, 102n26, 103n31
Transfer networks. *See* Payment systems, international

U.S.-Canada free-trade agreement (1988), 6, 21, 28
U.S. Department of the Treasury
effect of assistance to deposit insurance system, 83
relationship of central bank to, 90–94
Upham, Cyril B., 101n7

Vachon, Serge, 168

Walter, Ingo, 76n1
Willig, Robert, 36
Wire transfer insurance, 157
Wolf, Frederick, 102n21
Wriston, Walter, 65